More

Geral B

Awakening
the Healing Soul

"Geral's beautiful book truly bridges psychotherapy and indigenous practices, and all the while he has the great fortune of encountering himself. What amazing stories, adventures, transformations, healings, and, simply, reconnections! I love the way Geral presents indigenous people in such a straightforward way, with no idealization. As our modern world seeks better ways of healing, this insightful and lively book brings hope to the human family as it looks to Nature for balance and peace."

—FRANÇOISE BOURZAT, MA, author of *Consciousness Medicine*

"'Books, books, books, everywhere books,' remarks one of the indigenous healers with whom Geral Blanchard has connected. 'Much information. Not much wisdom.' This concise assessment of Western psychology teachings forms the basis of this volume.

"Blanchard transforms stories into powerful teachings. With a clear, accessible style, the reader can see far deeper into human experience than in most psychology textbooks today. More than simple description, Blanchard's purpose is to educate Westerners about indigenous healing. He is almost never at the center of his own writings, except as an example of the vulnerable experiences that Westerners must have if they are to move beyond learning into wisdom. Despite having traveled the world and written extensively on the topic, Blanchard remains humble to the core.

"How does one take a topic like the soul of healing without crushing it like a flower between the pages of a book? Unlike all too many

Western resources, Blanchard moves us beyond heart and soul and into the sacred."

—DAVID S. PRESCOTT, LICSW, author of *Feedback Informed Treatment in Clinical Practice*

"Timely, provocative, and exhilarating! Geral Blanchard reconnects traditional psychotherapy with the sacred art of healing through personal, elemental, and spiritual realms of consciousness. His stories of personal and patient healing reveal the deep truth of our own inner power to transform our lives. Merging Western medicine with indigenous wisdom, Blanchard gives birth to a new paradigm for practitioners to become midwives for their patients' healing as they awaken the 'shaman within.'"

—CARLENE MATTIMORE, LCPC, author of *Sacred Messages of Shamanic Africa*

Awakening
the Healing Soul

Awakening
the Healing Soul

Indigenous Wisdom for Today's World

GERAL T. BLANCHARD

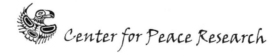

Center for Peace Research

To Emily, with heartfelt gratitude for spurring this cowboy forward on his most important call to adventure.

The situation that we now must deal with is not one of seeking the answer, but of facing the answer.

—Terence McKenna

Contents

Illustrations xiii

Acknowledgments xv

Introduction xvii

1 African Dreams, Sacred Magic,
   and the *Super Natural* 1

2 Transformation Begins 19

3 Health Crisis in the Amazon 29

4 The Heart of Bushman Spirituality and Healing . . . 54

5 A Primal Homecoming 74

6 Grounded on Mother Earth 81

7 Journey to the Land of Souls 94

8 Peruvian Plant-Medicine Shamanism 108

9 Ojibwa Healing of Interpersonal Violence 127

10 Grizzly Bear Medicine 147

11 The Psychedelic Revival 160

12 Traditional African Plant Medicines to Combat
    the Heroin Epidemic 176

13   Growing Beyond Self in Zimbabwe and Guatemala . . . 188

14   Healing Practices in Shamanism Worldwide 214

Conclusion 239

Appendix 249

Notes 255

Selected Bibliography 261

About the Author 265

Illustrations

FIGURES   **PAGE**

1   Mandaza Kandemwa   8

2   Visitation by Dove   10

3   P. H. Mtshali   13

4   Achuar Shaman Rafael   35

5   Reunion with Juan Fidel   51

6   Hadza Mother and Child Bonding   60

7   Q'ero Shaman, Peruvian Andes   109

8   Grizzly Bear   152

9   Baba Mandaza Making *Muti*   189

10 Victoria, the Maya Shaman, Lake Atitlan, Guatemala . . 202

11 Jaguar   206

12 Great Horned Owl   230

13 A Healing Mandala   233

14 Welcoming Ceremony, Venda Tribe, South Africa . . 245

TABLE

1   Two Diverse Systems of Accountability   146

xiii

Acknowledgments

I extend my great respect and gratitude to many indigenous teachers, two of whom were repeatedly referenced in this book: the late P. H. Mtshali, a Zulu sangoma from Swaziland; and Baba Mandaza Kandemwa, a Shona shaman, living in Zimbabwe. They sensed primal forces at work within me and respectfully exhorted me to wake up to the calling. Additionally, both men recognized a role that I could play in merging ancient and modern healing methods, a confidence that inspired me to pen this book.

Even before I met my African mentors many years ago, Burma Bushie, an Ojibwa elder in Manitoba, had patiently steered me onto a more traditionally grounded and sacred healing path that I will never abandon. She taught me how healers offer their best service to others when they are unafraid to listen to the ways of the heart and the whisperings of the soul. As best I am able, I am committed earnestly to embody Burma's humanistic philosophy, matched with her firebrand spirit, to bring profound changes to the healing arts and justice systems. Burma blurred boundaries in beautiful ways, convincing me how all animal endeavors—whether two-legged or four-legged—are forever relational and, therefore, sacred. Her accepting ways have consistently made me feel like an extended family member of Hollow Water First Nation, the Ojibwa community located on the east side of Lake Winnipeg, Canada.

So, I give great thanks to all the ancestors for showing up in their varied and interconnected forms, human brothers and sisters, the spirit of those who have passed and those yet to be born, and to other animal relatives—Grizzly, Margay, and Jaguar for starters. *Megwetch*!

I must also mention the anxiety I feel when a book comes down the birth canal. As with other authors, I might be perceived as a consummate expert in my area of professional fascination. At times that label can be a bit inaccurate and even intoxicating. But when my prejudices, writing errors, and other shortcomings are revealed during the editing process, a down-to-the-knees humility can quickly set in. That's when I prefer an editor who is not only a talented wordsmith with a sharp intellect but also someone who can gently correct me, again and again, without dousing my confidence and enthusiasm, and, at the same time, share my fervor for the project. And gently push me, too, when my interest predictably wanes, so that the prolonged labor of publishing will eventually lead to a joyous delivery. I found those talents in Sharron Dorr of Geneva, Illinois. I am very appreciative that she found me.

Introduction

Unprecedented advances in healing mind as well as body are now available through the blending of modern Western medicine with the ancient wisdom of indigenous healers who can still be found in remote corners of the world. I make this statement with confidence and conviction, being a Western-trained psychotherapist practicing in the United States who incorporates techniques I have learned firsthand from shamanistic healers of various cultures, from African to South American to Native North American. In this book, I recount some of my experiences with these healers and my use of their methods in my own psychotherapeutic practice. My goal is to communicate the vast potential for healing both psychological and physical ills that until now in our society has been largely untapped.

Serving the victims and perpetrators of violent crimes, I have worked as a psychotherapist in the field of interpersonal violence for over forty-five years. Some of my patients have included incarcerated pedophiles, rapists, and even the occasional serial killer and mass murderer. Other patients have suffered some of the most severe and chronic forms of trauma, or what experts refer to as *horiffica,* and such lingering psychological wounds regularly give rise to physical illnesses.

I learned a great deal about trauma and its aftermath while visiting Rwanda following the 1994 genocide and while visiting murderers on death row in the United States. My university training in psychology and anthropology, however, did not adequately prepare me for the full range of human complexity and suffering that I have encountered over the years of my career. And my formal education provided only a meager exoskeleton of best-practice and evidence-based guidelines that left little room for innovation and individualized care for my patients. Contemporary treatment modalities have too often created technical, mechanical, repetitious, and even monotonous approaches that were not tailored to meet the needs of the unique people sitting before me, whose circumstances were far outside the normal ranges of what my conventional training addressed.

During several trips to study indigenous populations throughout North America, I have witnessed many shamans healing patients without the availability of our Western arsenal of self-help books, pharmaceuticals, and modern clinics and hospitals. My eyes have been opened to new, yet old, ways of restoring harmony and health. Subsequently, I have broadened my exploration into indigenous cultures in Africa, South America, and Central America. Each exposure to traditional-medicine practices has deepened my belief in the inherent wisdom found in ancient approaches. I now believe that these approaches, which are estimated to have endured and been applied for forty-thousand years or more, should be considered *evidence based.* Too often, however, this worldwide ancient medicine is dismissed as *alternative*, whereas a medical innovation from ten years ago is considered *state-of-the-art* in our country!

In the following chapters, I will avoid painting a picture of indigenous healing in naïvely romantic ways; nor do I want to undermine confidence in the gifts of Western medicine. Rather, I want to examine indigenous wisdom in its true efficacy, understanding how far we have drifted from some of the most basic and artful skills ancient healers developed in the absence of neuroimaging devices, electroshock therapy, and the availability of inpatient psychiatric hospitals, Mayo Clinics, and Walgreens. Among the lost elements of healing are the use of personal beliefs and the power of the mind (i.e., the placebo effect), the knowledge and use of plant medicines, and soulful presence as medicine. Also important are thoughtfully orchestrated and dramatic rituals, community support, the careful infusion of sacred mystery, the power of presence and loving kindness, and many other factors that will become apparent through the true stories I relate in this book.

My goal is to bridge diverse cultures. Having my feet planted in both worlds—Western psychology and indigenous ways of knowing—I have been fortunate to experience personal healings from an Iowa surgeon and witnessed the disappearance of cancerous growths following shamanic treatments in the Amazon. Rather than offer a comparative view in predominantly dichotomous terms—old/new, scientific/superstitious, effective/ineffective, ethical/unethical—my intention is to create a fusion of skills. What I see as pertinent is a blend that doesn't reflexively move from trend to trend or advancement to advancement but reminds the reader of unchanging core principles and practices of healing that retain the human touch, the soul of healing. It would be unwise entirely to discount ancient methods because they seem exotic as well as entirely to disregard the role of pharmaceuticals amid the controversies swirling around Big Pharma. An open, informed, curious, and intuitive mind will become an innovative mind that can create an amalgam of techniques that, when delivered artfully, will optimize patient recovery.

Chapter 1, "African Dreams, Sacred Magic, and the *Super Natural*," recounts my first serious immersion into the world of *sangomas*, the Zulu term for "shamans," and shamanic healing in Africa. Two legendary traditional healers, Mandaza Kandemwa, a Shona water-spirits healer, and P. H. Mtshali, a Zulu sangoma, have left an indelible impression on my psyche that reset my healing compass.

Chapter 2, "Transformation Begins," tells the story of my reluctance fully to embrace the authenticity of many ancient forms of medicine after returning from Africa. Only when smacked in the face by a series of serendipitous moments did I finally suspend my disbelief and dramatically reshape my psychotherapy practice.

Chapter 3, "Health Crisis in the Amazon," recounts my experience of ministering to a dying Achuar man in the jungle of Ecuador. When the local shaman could not help the brain-injured man, the shaman convinced me that I had the skills to heal the man on the basis of a dream I had shared in the community's dream circle. The success I experienced in following indigenous healing methods took me to the next step of internalizing the ways of a natural healer.

In chapter 4, "The Heart of Bushman Spirituality and Healing," I describe the Hadza Bushmen of Tanzania. Their intimate grounding on the land with its plentiful medicines, matched with their quiet spirituality, makes every tribal member an effective healer. They heal each other. And, as they say, "healing others makes our hearts happy."

Chapter 5, "A Primal Homecoming," reveals the marked contrast between Western medicine and traditional healing that became increasingly evident to me after departing Africa and the Amazon. To be more effective as a psychotherapist, I came to the realization that it was imperative to deepen my harmonizing connections to the land and animals. As boundaries blurred among all sources of life energies, my healing work became more profound.

Chapter 6, "Grounded on Mother Earth," explores the natural path to being grounded on Mother Earth in a modern world. With an existence increasingly insulated from Nature, Western healers must find ways to reconnect with the healing energies the natural world provides. I explain the *earthing* movement, with its new/old technologies, that have their origins in Native American wisdom.

Chapter 7, "Journey to the Land of the Souls," demonstrates another bridge between ancient and modern medicines; it recounts my visit to Hollow Water—an Ojibwa First Nation Reserve in Manitoba, Canada—and the story of a traumatized Ojibwa teenager who facilitated his own healing with the help of modern neurotechnology. I stress the importance of commencing healing ceremonies by fostering an altered state, in this case with a brain-stimulation device. Traveling to distant places in his mind, the young man was reunited with his deceased parents and sister and recovered from the pain of his traumatic loss.

Chapter 8, "Peruvian Plant-Medicine Shamanism," features the healing powers of a Shipibo shaman in Peru who restored the hearing of my traveling companion after he had lost much of his hearing over the years. My companion was introduced to jungle medicines and rituals which, almost immediately, stimulated a reconfiguration of the inner ear and enhanced his auditory perceptiveness.

Chapter 9, "Ojibwa Healing of Interpersonal Violence," takes the reader back to the Ojibwa First Nation Reserve in Manitoba. After many visits to Hollow Water, I had become intimately familiar with the community's successful method of addressing sexual abuse. Moving away from the pathologizing habits of white psychologists, and by discarding many of the punitive and isolating law-enforcement practices, the Ojibwa had reintroduced previously suppressed spiritual values and traditional remedies community wide. The results were stunning and enhanced an international movement toward restorative justice—or what Corrections Canada, the Canadian federal-government agency, calls "satisfying justice."

"Grizzly-Bear Medicine" is the subject and title of chapter 10. Indigenous cultures on both the North American and the Asian continents have long recognized the healing power of Brown Bear. By ritualistically merging grizzly energy with the attenuated energy of wounded humans, strength is acquired that helps to surmount both psychological and physical maladies.

Chapter 11, "The Psychedelic Revival," speaks to the current renewal of interest in psychotropic substances that first appeared in the United States in the 1960s. Ayahuasca, iboga, kratom, mushrooms, cactus, and even toads are enjoying a newly cleansed reputation because of their profound, research-observed effectiveness in resolving trauma, addictions, and many other mental-health problems. Matched with modern pharmaceuticals such as MDMA and ketamine, and when coupled with indigenous rituals, we now have a wide array of promising medicines that are providing astonishing relief for thousands of suffering souls.

Chapter 12, "Traditional African Plant Medicines to Combat the Heroin Epidemic," addresses the global heroin epidemic and the dangers of Big Pharma "remedies" for opioid addictions. Today it is considered best practice to treat heroin addiction with pharmaceuticals that are far more addictive than virtually all other opioids. When used in the proper set and setting,[1] the African root, *iboga,* and the Malaysian leaf, *kratom,* offer astonishing relief from these addictions without creating new addictions.

Chapter 13, "Growing beyond Self In Zimbabwe and Guatemala," explores the indigenous cosmovisions from far-flung locations on two continents that focus on the underlying unity of all people, beyond local and national tribal identities. Echoing the teachings of Mahatma Gandhi and His Holiness the Dalai Lama, this transcendent view comprises a consciousness of the One Spirit as a unifying energy that moves through all beings and all things. To heal people, the importance of "dying to ego," or self-importance, in the service of this great mystery while harmoniously unifying with all life forms is the central message of shamans everywhere. Embracing the truth of One Consciousness is an all-purpose medicine.

Chapter 14, "Healing Practices in Shamanism Worldwide," examines the common elements utilized by indigenous healers worldwide. Almost all shamans emphasize the power of ceremony and ritual, mystery, sacred magic, altered states, and authorita-tiveness to lift people into higher-vibratory healing dimensions. Additionally, softer qualities such as humility, full attention, love, and the potentiating power of a community's embrace make for the best practice in whatever culture a healer resides.

The conclusion is that we can't throw the baby out with the bathwater. Ancient and modern healing approaches often comingle quite well, but this requires an artful approach, not just mechanical technologies. My hope is that this book makes such an approach more accessible both for healers and for those they would help.

1

African Dreams, Sacred Magic, and the *Super Natural*

One afternoon in the spring of 2005, I began to understand the important distinction between the terms *supernatural* and *super natural.* An unexpected phone call prompted a string of decisions that would irrevocably change the trajectory of my career and my life, as well as raise my awareness that the healing powers found in Nature offer super medicines. A Canadian friend reached out to propose an academic study that seemed both idyllic and timely. He was planning a unique sojourn to southern Africa with the intent of studying shamanism. Participation would be limited to four people—a university instructor, a botanist, a spiritual healer, and perhaps a psychotherapist such as me—who would witness traditional healing practices in several countries. After I promised to deliberate carefully over the offer and respond within a few days, the truth was I knew within minutes that this was a trip I would undertake. Intuition—a deep inner calling—advised me that this journey would be imperative and a way I could unfold into a more authentic version of myself and become a better healer. Upon arising the next morning, the first thing I did was to formalize my commitment to travel with the group. It was an urgent decision from the heart that no financial or health considerations were going to derail. I imagined a grandfatherly Joseph Campbell overseeing my deliberation while nudging me forward. Most assuredly Joe would have said, "Follow your bliss."

Reaching Our Destination

Just a couple months later, our unique contingent was greeted by a Venda tribal shaman at the Johannesburg airport. He would serve as interpreter and guide throughout our travels. Ramaliba was dressed in a tattered and ill-fitting sport coat that had seen better days. His attire was a thoughtful gesture of respect, as he had dressed in a way that he determined was befitting for meeting North Americans. Within minutes we were seated in a van embarking on a long drive across South Africa, heading toward his healing compound just south of the Zimbabwe border.

En route we were alerted to the Venda custom of honoring special visitors with a potentially long and elaborate greeting. Indeed, that was the case. The welcome—including a full night of ingesting alcoholic beverages followed by many hours of drumming and dancing, the slaughter of a goat, feasting, and visiting tribal dignitaries the next day, all with no sleep—was totally exhausting, especially as it was preceded by two flights across the United States, a trans-Atlantic flight, a final, arduous leg from Paris to the southern tip of Africa, and all the hours of ground transportation that came afterward.

After we had spent days exploring healing in the Venda culture, Ramaliba served as our guide to Zimbabwe to meet with the renowned Mandaza Kandemwa, a Shona water-spirits healer. Entering the country and traveling during the dark of night proved to be harrowing. Just crossing the border from South Africa was an ordeal, with hours of delays, being separated from one another, and not knowing if or when we would meet again. The stress and fear were so intense that one traveler in our group quickly developed stomach and intestinal problems. Finally, when all government suspicions of nefarious travel intentions were eliminated in our separate interviews, we were greatly relieved to be reunited and back on the road again. And traveling late at night, twice our vehicle was halted by gun-toting men, poorly disguised as police. Thanks to our guide, Ramaliba, a degree of cajoling and a payment of rands (the South African currency) allowed us to continue our journey.

The Shona Cosmovision

At last we arrived at our destination—the Zimbabwean town of Bulywayo. As soon as our gear was unpacked the first evening, I found myself sitting on a log with Mandaza, gazing at a beautiful starlit sky with the Southern Cross above us. Immediately he began sharing the Shona cosmovision and healing tenets. Other shamans were drawn to Mandaza's home by his personal invitation and by their private dreams that had alerted them to our arrival. They wanted to meet their Western colleagues who shared enthusiasm for their traditional healing approaches.

In much of rural Africa, it is a shamanic practice each morning to form a circle to recount and interpret dreams of the previous night. And so we did, eight of us from four countries. Among many indigenous cultures, dreams are regarded as the raw and true reality. By contrast, our waking existence—referred to as a "cultural nightmare" by one of the traditional healers—is regarded as a filtered and adulterated realm distorted by social influences. Dreams are believed to be important harbingers. Once their guiding messages are unwrapped and understood, they must be acted upon immediately. In the Shona culture, dreams are an important way in which individuals receive messages from the sacred domain, a realm that is parallel to the world of the living. Dreams can guide shamans to healing cures. Often an ancestor who has passed over will offer advice to a shaman in a dream, whether in sleep, in a lucid, semiawake state, or during trance possession. Another belief is that dreams serve to validate our underlying emotional experience and that emotions carry messages. At a minimum, the content of dreams, with their attendant emotions, can suggest that we have remaining personal work to complete in our current lives.

When it came to be my turn to speak in the dream circle, I asked if it was permissible to "pass." I felt my dream was so mundane that it didn't merit discussion. The shamans looked somewhat askance at my request. Why would I decline to share something as important as my dream content? Upon the group's insistence, I reluctantly explained that I had dreamt of shopping for office supplies in a Wyoming Walmart when I coincidentally bumped into some old friends. Immediately, the dream's importance and its portent were obvious to the healers, and with a few clarifying questions, it was interpreted for me. I had been so wrapped up in my customary work pattern, they surmised, that my evenings and even my dream life were driven by work obligations. I was told that this habit caused me to neglect important social ties and friendships. I was meeting friends only by happenstance rather than by plan. And how is it, they pondered, that a healer could serve his patients well if friends were not available to support and minister to him? Busted!

Water-Spirits Initiation

On my first full day in Zimbabwe, Mandaza directed me to sit at the foot of a tree and ask, "How might I serve you?"

"And how long should I do this?" I inquired.

He responded, "Most of this day. Then we will talk."

I grumbled to myself, wondering if I had traveled this far simply to talk to a tree. As it turned out, repeating that mantra for many hours made me aware that my sacred worldly role is to be of service—to everyone and all life forms. My task as a healer, Mandaza stressed, was to diminish self or ego as some separate entity and see the interconnectedness of all beings, all things. I recalled the Prayer of Saint Francis of Assisi, who said, "Grant that I may not so much seek to be consoled as to console . . . for it is in giving that we receive." Once I had grasped the full import of the assigned query, Mandaza was satisfied that he could share tribal-healing information with me and begin the water-spirits' initiation rituals.

The following morning, I awakened to find a mysterious, if not eerie-looking, woman sleeping on the grass outside Mandaza's house. The day before our arrival, a dream had revealed to her that several foreign healers were coming to Bulywayo, and she requested to meet with all of us. She had hiked into town to meet us. Soon I was summoned to Mandaza's healing room behind his living quarters. There was the mysterious and somewhat frightening-looking woman. Identified by Mandaza as a shaman, she was now lying on the concrete floor, eyes rolled back in an altered state, snarling like a leopard. She had shapeshifted; it was the first of my several exposures to different shamans who had this fascinating ability to enter other realities, to merge with animal guardians, and to exit those realms under their own volition.

After coming out of the trance and returning to human posture and voice, she asked two things of me, Mandaza serving as the interpreter: "Why do you live so far away from your son? And what happened to that silver ring that is always on the second finger of your right hand?"

Whoa! Where had *that* come from? Indeed, I did live nine hours by car from my adult son, which prohibited frequent visits. And, in fact, I did customarily wear a silver, elk-tooth ring on my right hand, but I had decided not to wear any jewelry on this trip to Africa. I began to feel unsettled.

Next the woman inquired, "What about the little girl . . . ?" and then quickly checked her speech, as if deciding that it would be inappropriate to pursue the subject any further. I suddenly felt even more unsettled, wondering what she was suggesting. Was she somehow aware of the little girl I once sought to adopt, only to learn later that she was murdered by her natural parents? Only a few people knew about that part of my life in the 1970s.

Her inquiries were interrupted by Mandaza, who said it was time to step outside where he could begin introducing all of us to the water spirits' healing tradition of his tribe. I was directed to the bank of a shallow, muddy pool of water. It appeared as though the mysterious female shaman was going to engage in some of the activities with us. As would occur many times in the days to come, I was left hanging, asking myself, "What is about to happen?" and "What just happened?" As soon as questions came to mind, we would be swept away into other equally confounding rituals. It was a whirlwind of mysterious activities, much of it going without explanation or interpretation, leaving me to sift through the experience for months and years later.

The Shona tribe is part of the large Bantu-language group. Mandaza lives out his cultural heritage with pride and reveres his power connections with Africa's lions and leopards. The water spirits, however, are the most influential guiding agents of all. Like angels, they are said to come from Creator. And water spirits have the greatest wisdom and healing energy. Mandaza was quietly proud to share this sacred part of his culture with us.

It was time for me to be submerged into a pool of water as part of my initiation into the water spirits' healing tradition. First, I had to ingest a handful of termite dung. After I had been choking on it for at least fifteen minutes, Mandaza then filled my other hand with something else to be licked and swallowed. This time he chose not to tell me of the contents, having seen my revolted reaction to the first handful of *muti* (medicine). Then a white liquid was whipped into a froth, and dollops were placed over my torso.

With that, I was led to the water with the female shaman shadowing my every step. Apparently, she had decided to submerge herself with me, which was an unnerving prospect, given her mysterious nature. But because I had formed an immediate trust for Mandaza, and noting that he showed no hesitation over her participation, I did not object.

FIGURE 1. Mandaza Kandemwa. This Shona water-spirits healer of Zimbabwe reveres his power connections with lions and leopards. (Author's photograph)

Instructed to hold my breath for as long as I could, I slid under the water's surface, only to feel the woman's hands on my body. I began trembling and, unable to hold my breath for more than a few short seconds, burst upward out of the water. There stood Mandaza on the bank with an approving smile. Three more times he signaled for me to enter the water, and each time I could only hold my breath for a few seconds before strong tremors resumed. Mandaza addressed me as "Sea Lion" and invited me to step out of the pool and sit down in the sunlight.

In many indigenous cultures, Mandaza explained, convulsions of this kind are signs that a shamanic transformation is unfolding. With that encouraging insight, I sat down under a warming sun and closed my eyes. That is when amazing visions began to appear! Images of African animals, one by one, came into focus until every detail, every whisker and eyelash, were crisp and clear. After a few moments, each animal would slowly fade out of focus while another took its place, becoming sharper and sharper. Every animal presented itself in side profile, with only one eye revealed. And to my bewilderment, each appeared to have a slight simper on its face. Some of the primates were rare animals—ones that I had seldom seen before departing on the trip. Amazed by the realistic nature of the visions, I briefly opened my eyes to orient myself to space and time. When I closed my eyes again in comforting reassurance of my sanity, the parade of animals resumed. I continued to be able to enter into and remove myself from the visions at will. Later, Mandaza told me that the intent of the ceremony was to develop my third eye—an intuitive way of seeing and knowing—so that I could move in and out of different realities with the help of African animal spirits, much as he did.

Later that day, while I was listening to Mandaza speak of peace at the entryway of one of his healing huts, a white Zimbabwean dove descended from the sky and landed on his shoulder. Mandaza seemed nonplussed and continued to speak without interruption. I summoned a colleague, instructing him to locate my camera quickly so that I could capture the moment. Just as he returned with camera in hand, a second dove arrived and landed atop my head. If it were not for the photos that captured the event, I wondered if anyone back home in Wyoming would believe my account. The approving animal world was joining us in many ways during this reverent time.

FIGURE 2. Visitation by Dove. The bird landed on my head just as Mandaza was talking about peace. (Author's photograph)

The Call of a Dream

On the third morning in Zimbabwe, the dream circle assembled as usual. Ramaliba opened it with eagerness. I discovered that he was a robust dreamer who always kept a journal by his bed, recording his dreams throughout the night before they could fade away. The previous evening, he had dreamt of an old Zulu man from Swaziland named Mtshali. The man was said to be seriously ill and needed muti of a kind that only Ramaliba could concoct. Ramaliba insisted that we immediately pack our bags and follow his guiding dream to Swaziland. That is how things work in Africa; you don't doubt the message held in carefully interpreted dreams, as the veil between different realities is relatively seamless.

No sooner had we arrived in Zimbabwe than we were off to points unknown, with no address and no phone number to determine our final destination in Swaziland. Traveling down the roadways for the next two days, we picked up animal and plant materials that were stuffed into our van—all ingredients for Mtshali's muti. Following the guidance of ancestors who communicated to him in his dream, Ramaliba gathered elephant dung, a dead owl, nuts, and leaves from tree branches. They would be combined to form a concoction designed to heal the stranger identified in the dream as Mtshali, whose exact disease had yet to be revealed to the rest of us.

First, we passed through Ramaliba's Venda community, where he stopped at his plant-medicine hut to assemble the final essential ingredients for the muti. He stayed awake throughout the night tending a fire under a large, round, black kettle—boiling and stirring the ingredients and then waiting for them to cool before storing muti in old Fanta soda bottles. During the night, Ramaliba also made a concoction for me, explaining that it would improve my overall energy, which he observed was low. I was to keep my soda bottle close by during our travels and periodically take swigs from it, until the two-liter bottle of liquid mud was emptied. I was somewhat surprised by my ability to get past the initial disgusting taste and eventually savor the earthy muti, trusting that it would be good medicine. To my satisfaction, I rapidly felt invigorated.

As the sun began to rise the next morning, we were off to Swaziland again. By late afternoon we crossed the border into Zulu territory without incident or delay. The presentation of Ramaliba's passport, along with the announcement that he was a shaman arriving to treat a patient, was satisfying enough to scoot us through the immigration station. When we were approaching the mountains near the community of Siteki, which is close to the Mozambique border, Ramaliba's excitement grew as he recognized that he was near the destination seen in his dream. With darkness coming, Ramaliba asked our driver to pull over again and again so that he could knock on the doors of the *rondavels* (circular huts) to solicit detailed directions. No one was familiar with the name *Mtshali*. Many women seemed frightened by the very tall, heavy, bald-headed Venda man at their door. After observing the futility of the door-to-door search for information on Mtshali's specific place of residence, I offered words of advice to my traveling companions.

"In my culture," I said, "frightening people in the dark of night is impolite."

Ramaliba, without defensiveness, replied, "In Venda culture, to let an ill person die is impolite."

Point taken! We drove on into the night. Just after midnight, near the summit of a mountain facing Mozambique, a tiny fence sign appeared on the side of the road. It read "P. H. Mtshali."

"That's it!" our driver exclaimed, and Ramaliba leaned over to honk the horn repeatedly. I checked myself before offering more advice on politeness.

A barefoot, elderly man quickly scampered toward us and immediately asked if we were the ones bringing him muti for his breathing problems. Ramaliba presented the pop bottle and, without hesitation, Mtshali gulped down some of the thick brew, fully trusting the intuitive nature of African healing. The dream world always gets things right.

We were invited to bed down on his property and ended up staying for two days treating Mtshali's lung problems; he was having great difficulty breathing. We watched his energy and breath strengthen hour by hour. As a gracious host, he somehow summoned the energy to speak about his culture and Zulu healing philosophy. He was, in fact, a traditional healer, too, and a highly respected one. In Africa, shamans heal shamans. And in

FIGURE 3. P. H. Mtshali. A traditional healer himself, Mtshali was wise on the subject of Zulu healing philosophy. (Author's photograph)

Zulu culture, shamans are referred to as *sangomas*, a term that meant nothing to me at the time but later would prove to be of utmost personal importance.

Mtshali advised us that Western medicine was so research oriented that little value was placed on personal experience. He explained that in the West unrelated people—usually total strangers not connected by blood, community, or dreams—are presumed to know what is best for them. Additionally, the power of mystery is underestimated in the West and isn't considered as a valuable component of the healing equation. Most importantly, he insisted, love has to be injected into the healing process. A sangoma must first love himself. From that secure spot, he or she can fully love others and, ultimately, with that powerful muti in the heart, is best able to heal patients.

After witnessing Mtshali's vitality being restored during our brief stay, we planned to depart after the second full day on the mountain. I was the first person to climb into the van, restless as usual, awaiting our departure for the next adventure. In a not-so-fast mode, Mtshali summoned me back to his healing rondavel. That was a surprise. Sensing something important was about to occur, I grabbed my journal and summoned our botanist, and together we went to the hut. Upon entering the circular, one-room structure, I immediately noted the presence of some unfamiliar faces, including three sangomas who were sitting in a circle with Mtshali. At home, a surprise gathering like this would have felt like a chemical-dependency intervention. I glanced in the direction of my colleague, signaling that I needed her eyes and ears. She nodded in return while removing a journal from her backpack, tacitly assuring me that she would be an astute observer of the intrigue that was unfolding.

At first it seemed as if Mtshali was going to spend some perfunctory time thanking me for visiting him. Later I realized that there is nothing cursory or superficial about the man. Mtshali reached for a water-buffalo scrotum that was filled with an amalgam of bones and a few other symbolic items—from dominos to what appeared to be a G. I. Joe figure. He asked me to blow my personal life force (breath) into the mix and then rolled the bones out on the mat separating us—a divination process known as "throwing the bones." Four times I repeated the ritual. Each time I noticed the other sangomas were carefully taking note of the order in which the items landed on the mat and the relationship of each object to the others. They conferred as a group, validating some sort of shared conclusion drawn from the configuration.

Then a female sangoma, who was seated immediately to my left and spoke English, whispered into my ear, advising me to pay close attention to a message Mtshali was receiving. He smiled broadly and began laughing in a high-pitched voice. He announced that he was speaking to my deceased maternal grandmother. She reportedly was happy to see me again after her death decades earlier. He was amused by my grandmother's surprise that I would appear to her in the company of black Zulu healers in Africa. Mtshali took seriously a complaint from her that I had failed to decorate my home with the decorative doilies she had made for me after I had purchased my first home. He was befuddled that I wasn't honoring my deceased ancestor by placing her handiwork around the house. He didn't ask for corroboration; he just had a knowing that the information he was receiving was, indeed, accurate. I didn't know what to make of these specific revelations.

As suddenly as the laughter had commenced, it ceased just as abruptly. The emotional atmosphere inside the rondavel shifted. Once again, the female sangoma advised me to be very attentive to what was about to be revealed. Mtshali asked when I would be returning home to the United States. I roughed out our schedule and the anticipated departure time. He deliberated and reassuringly indicated that it would be soon enough. Soon enough for what, I wondered? Mtshali soberly announced that my mother was dying and that my father was seriously ill and in a hospital too. I was needed at home and had to make peace with both of them, particularly my father. Mtshali acknowledged that a longstanding tension existed between my father and me but said it was now time to put acrimony to rest, for our mutual benefit.

This art of communicating with spirits of the dead and prophesizing the future—a practice common among African traditional healers—is referred to as *necromancy*. Mtshali treats the dead as just another "age group." I wasn't impressed with his purported abilities at the time. My rational, skeptical, and cynical mind presumed that this was just some kind of showmanship on his part. It would be a year before I received clarity in this regard.

As we were about to part company, Mtshali had some words of encouragement for me. With his eyes closed, he explained how he was scanning my Wyoming office with his mind's eye.

"Books, books, books, everywhere books," he remarked. "Much information. Not much wisdom."

From the perspective of his eighty years on this earth, Mtshali believed that my redemption and growth would occur once I spent more time communicating with the ancestors and engaged in more traditional healing experiences with my patients.

He said, "I envy you, Gerry. This next year will be important for you," implying that I would partake of many exciting and informative healing experiences. His parting words to me were, "Soon you will be a sangoma."

His prophecy meant little to me at the time. For one thing, I didn't even know what the term *sangoma* meant. I would likely have forgotten it had my colleague not written it down. I was so consumed with the messages pertaining to my parents' ill health that my focus went exclusively to them. And, I must admit, I felt some confusion and even a little animosity toward Mtshali, thinking that perhaps he was playing me a bit.

Before we parted, Mtshali instructed me to go to the local outdoor market and look for a white cloth, something that looked like what my grandma called a doily, and place it at the foot of my bed. Next, he told me to look for a *kente* cloth, a multicolored cloth, long and narrow, that he insisted I wrap around my father's neck while hugging him and apologizing for being gone so much. Mtshali said I should leave it with my father, so that any time he missed me he could wrap it around his neck and remember my hug.

The doily, I presumed, would be a difficult order to fill. Not so. The first vendor I encountered immediately upon entering the local market had a three-foot long, white woven cloth on display, front and center. The woman sitting behind the table looked at me and then pointed to the cloth, saying, "You need this." Of course, I did. And I purchased it. Later I came across a brightly colored kente cloth and set it aside for my father.

Many other interesting encounters with shamans occurred as we traveled through southern Africa. None of them, however, were as poignant and influential as my time with Mandaza

Kandemwa and P. H. Mtshali. They were not merely ceremo-nialists and herbalists, vessels of knowledge about plants and rituals. Both men were very generous, reverent, expressive, and loving individuals who viewed their time with patients as sacred service. They left a deep and lasting impression.

Transformation
Begins

A week passed after my private meeting with Mtshali and before our group departed Johannesburg. As soon as I arrived in Newark, I turned on my cell phone and placed a call to one of my sisters. She urgently announced that my mother had just undergone cataract surgery in Minnesota when her heart began beating very erratically. Quickly she had been sent to a cardiologist and was prepped for surgery, and an electric stimulator was implanted. While a Mayo Clinic hospitalist was examining her a few days later, cancer was detected—fourth-stage cancer that had spread throughout her body. Mother's time on this earth, the Western doctor projected, would be short. A traditional healer might have likened this type of prognostic assessment to a hex. In response, Mother had resigned herself to the inevitability of imminent death.

"And Dad?" I inquired of my sister. "How is he?"

She explained that he, too, was seriously ill and had been hospitalized with pneumonia atop his chronic challenges with Parkinson's disease. I immediately went to Minnesota to be close to both my parents.

Mother died soon after my arrival, with several of her children at her side, comforted in part by the knowledge that her mother had just been present with Mtshali and me in Africa. With her solid Christian beliefs, Mother departed this realm in the hope that she would be in the company of Grandma very soon, much as she understood I had been.

Weeks later, upon following Mtshali's advice on how to approach my father apologetically and affectionately for being absent for many years, I went to Dad's nursing care facility. Walking into his room unannounced, I was prepared to do all the talking, having been informed that his voice had been reduced to just a faint whisper. Tilted to his side in a recliner adjacent to his bed, and with the typical expressionless face of a Parkinson's patient, Father's eyes opened wide as he saw me walk into the room.

Somehow, he managed to straighten himself up and in a clear and very discernable voice exclaimed, "Geral!"

I hugged him and wrapped the African kente cloth around his neck saying, as per Mtshali's guidance, "I am sorry for having been gone so long. Anytime you want a hug from me, just wrap this cloth around your shoulders."

It was a comforting moment for both of us, and, surprisingly, the very next day I saw my father at a public outing with the cloth draped around him. He was rejuvenated enough for a social outing. Both of us were healing.

Work Becomes Service

Thereafter, I continued my psychotherapy practice in Wyoming, routinely reflecting on my time in Swaziland with Mtshali and many other shamans. As I lectured across the United States, I noticed that my African experiences would regularly percolate to the surface and find their way into my talks. It was not always consciously planned, but I was clearly being guided in that direction. I began emphasizing the importance of integrating ancient healing traditions with modern counseling approaches—including in neuroscientific modalities and even in biochemical mental health interventions. Each talk increasingly emphasized the sacred nature of the healing process. Audiences favorably responded to my message. Occasionally, workshop attendees would arise during my lectures and ask for help with personal problems, physical and emotional. While speaking I would demonstrate, quite academically, how to blend ancient and modern healing practices, only to see dramatic recoveries being reported in front of everyone.

These incidents were not something to which I was accustomed. In fact, at first the exchanges left me feeling awkward and unsettled, even mildly embarrassed. I worried that my presentations would not be taken seriously, that I might be coming across like a fundamentalist religious healer conducting an event that resembled a tent revival. It seemed as though too much attention was being directed toward me personally, and the information I was trying to impart was becoming somewhat secondary. I also felt in myself an inclination to dismiss, or at least to minimize, some of the transformative healings that were occurring around me. And these healings were happening not just at communal gatherings but during my private-practice sessions as well. I reflected on previous admonitions from both Mtshali and Mandaza that a sacred healer is always to remain humble, knowing that it is the spirits, the patient, and a supportive community that activate the inner healer who slumbers in many people. Shamans are merely the choreographers of ceremonial events until spirits are summoned to do the big work.

The Utah Awakening

After traveling to many parts of the United States in the year following my introduction to traditional African healers, I arrived at a ski resort in the Wasatch Mountains of Utah, where I was scheduled to address two back-to-back conferences of psychotherapists, social workers, and psychologists. As was now becoming customary, my lectures gravitated toward the reverent nature of indigenous medicine and how well those methods could complement contemporary Western approaches. The audiences remained enthusiastic; in fact, two individuals insisted on receiving some personal attention while I spoke, wanting to be treated in a way that would showcase the sacred practices of traditional healers. Both healers themselves, they seemed poised for recovery and were choosing the circumstances, the methodology, and the facilitator that felt right for them to take an immediate step toward improved health. Hearing no objections from the remainder of the audience, I began serving each person—blending the old with the new, the clinically mechanical with the mysteriously sacred—while they felt focused support and care emanating from their colleagues.

As had consistently been the case over the year since returning from Africa, the results were positive and dramatic—what, as I have mentioned, I would later term *super natural*. The phenomenon was still quite surprising to me at the time, although it was intuitively anticipated by the patients. Echoing in my mind were the words of Robert Chambers, a mideighteenth-century author. In his book, *Vestiges of Creation,* he wrote, "The term *supernatural* is a gross mistake. We have to enlarge our conceptions of the natural, and all will be right." According to traditional healers, very frequently significant and immediate outcomes occur when patients are in a participatory role with the healer while engaged in a carefully orchestrated and compassionate ceremony supported by community involvement. Then, when the patient and healer's belief systems are aligned, virtually anything is possible. That is a natural—or *super natural*—phenomenon that has been observed for centuries in indigenous cultures.

As the second conference entered its final day, I felt uncomfortable and overwhelmed, as if a bright spotlight was shining on me. Feeling increasingly uneasy, I asked the organizer to move me from the beautiful mountain resort to downtown Salt Lake City where I could find privacy in a hotel room and reflect on what was happening—not just that week, but over the entire previous year of my life. He was understanding of my request and kindly obliged. Retiring to a downtown hotel, I pulled the curtains of my room together, allowing myself to go inward. I collapsed on the bed.

But before much time had passed, I grew restless. I felt compelled to go for a walk, deciding to look for the comfort of a bookstore or a coffee shop. Books had always been my close companions, especially when they grounded me in comforting facts that arose from outside myself. Perhaps, though, as Mtshali had cautioned, they were distracting me from the important, personal, and powerful life experiences unfolding all around me. Nevertheless, I headed out. And while walking, I recollected that it had been twelve months since I had departed Swaziland and my sangoma mentor, Mtshali. Indeed, it had been that long since he proclaimed that in the year following our providential meeting many transformative events would unfold, experiences he would likely envy. *Envy*, I once again pondered? And he also conveyed that one day I would realize that, like him, I, too, would follow the sangoma's healing path, a wonderful opportunity as he knew it.

As I was walking through downtown Salt Lake City, *voilà*! Before me was a very large, used bookstore with a coffee shop just inside the front door. I entered and ordered an Americano. The first section of books I encountered was tidily filled, floor to ceiling, with books on Native American culture. At waist level there was a protruding shelf where you could rest your coffee cup or books. It was completely bare except for one book, seemingly out of its proper place. I immediately approached it and noticed the African design on its cover. The title sent a shiver through me: *Sangoma*! I read the jacket, which summarized the story of a Midwestern man, James Hall, who unexpectedly found himself in Swaziland with a sangoma (not Mtshali) who threw the bones, spoke with Hall's ancestors, and surmised that he, too, would one day become a sangoma. Indeed, Hall did just that, even moving to Swaziland to follow his bliss. Opening the front cover, I saw that the price of the book was marked at half price. Another sign? I wondered. Given Mtshali's previous caution about my excessive reliance on book knowledge over personal experience, I wondered if he would approve of me purchasing still another book, especially this one. Of course he would, I concluded, given the topic and how I had long been predisposed to learn about it; this book was a tailored way to reach me with an important message. A clarion call of sorts.

I noted the apparent "massive coincidence" (a concept I no longer use) before me and immediately bought the book and returned to my hotel room to devour it. In a couple of hours, I had finished reading it, noting the incredible synchronicities between Hall and me. Because his story was almost identical to mine, great confusion and even a little paranoia swept over me. I distrustfully wondered if all Zulu sangomas stroke the egos of visiting Americans by saying the very same thing—that they will become traditional healers one day. Do we all desperately need to feel special in that way, with some of us striking out to follow the sangoma suggestions? But how did Mtshali know all the details about my grandmother, my mother, my father, and my office space and personal foibles?

My discomfort precipitated a phone call. I reached out to a spiritually minded friend from the Ojibwa Hollow Water First Nation Reservation in Manitoba. During the call I spent extensive time summarizing the story of my life over the last year, sharing many details. I clarified how confused and even somewhat frightened I was by how each and every sequential event seemed to be arranged by some kind of divine ordinance. My friend patiently listened for at least half an hour and then announced how puzzled he was, not by the events, but by my reaction to them. He reduced the situation down to some basic Ojibwa common sense.

He said, "In our culture, healing has always been seen as a good thing. I suggest you enjoy it. Bye-bye."

At first his terseness seemed insensitive and dismissive. It certainly wasn't what I desired, so impulsively I decided to call him again. But after a brief pause for reflection, I realized that his words rang true. How could healing, especially if done with loving, clear intentions and in a sacred way, be anything but good?

At that point, it became clear just what Mtshali's remark about envy meant. I was approaching something bigger and better than I had ever known before. He had been thinking about me "coming into my own," anticipating the year after my departure from Africa. No subtle hint was going to capture my attention; I needed a sacred two-by-four to the head, lovingly administered in a bookstore and by a distant good friend. Finally, revelations were coming in an entirely unambiguous way so that they could be absorbed—the appearance of a perfectly positioned book at the exact time it was needed—as I was opening up to the salience of traditional healing.

Shifting Values

Over the next two years, I reflected on my psychotherapy practice and the associates who worked under my supervision. Too often I felt as if our office had taken on the features of a cattle yard. We herded people together in a lobby and funneled them into counselors' offices for their magical fifty-minute treatment. Then, with a payment ritual that was never overlooked, patients were sent on their way until the next session. To be painfully candid, it was beginning to feel profane.

After my poignant visit to southern Africa in 2008, I left my conventional counseling office in Wyoming to develop a more reverent, attentive, and indigenous-influenced practice in the Midwest. Today, when a patient requests it, their healing is interspersed with ceremonies, rituals, and ancient healing approaches that, for each of us, often arise intuitively. I am no longer locked into any generic, one-size-fits-all set of protocols that are currently regarded as *best practice* or *evidence based* in the confining Western sense.

There is much wisdom to be garnered from the forty thousand years of priestly shamanism that has endured to this day in a few distant and remote locations. Traditional medicine is now experiencing a revitalization and is being adapted in a variety of forms in the West. I have learned that each patient session must be tailored to meet each person's unique psychological, physical, and spiritual needs. Most of all, though, each must be aligned with the patient's own belief system and cultural cosmovision. In my practice, most patients are now being encouraged to help craft their own treatment plans with the modalities they are comfortable having applied. My old allegiance to the unquestioned supremacy of the Western paradigm's scientific, rational, technological, rigid, and depersonalized methods have started to give way. Today, I can place trust in many elements that are invisible and mysterious, and I have a greater appreciation for the powerful healing that can arise from immeasurable, inexplicable, and ineffable sources.

Once my life had been impacted by the sacred influence of indigenous teachers, there would be no return to my former narrow dimensions. Maybe, just maybe, the universe doesn't always follow a mechanical and totally predictable clockwork pattern; nor is it simply chaotic and random. In unique and sometimes discomforting ways, it may be guiding its inhabitants to exactly where they need to go—if we are willing to listen. Today, I encourage patients to look beyond limiting concepts such as fate and destiny, inviting them to become *meaning makers* and, in an evolutionary sense, *cocreators* of their lives. A like-minded colleague refers to this process as a *future retrieval*.

Health Crisis
in the Amazon

When I position myself in the Office of Nature, especially when surrounded by indigenous people, another facet of my healing practice often emerges. I become far more open-minded, innovative, and spontaneous. It is as if I am being guided by a quiet *knowing*, as if I am being steered by an underlying energetic reality, tapping into patterns of which I am only faintly aware on a conscious level. Call it the "collective unconscious" as the depth psychologist C. G. Jung did, or the "shaman within" that is no longer smothered and stifled by university training. That latent part of myself may be what Jung called "the two-million-year-old man" who resides in all of us.[1] Amid that continuous, unbroken life force, knowledge is carried forward, generation to generation, at an unconscious level. When a healer is liberated from the shackles of narrow healing paradigms, an optimal healing spirit can suddenly and quite unexpectedly emerge. With that newfound freedom, a latent power is rediscovered that better enables us to facilitate patient recovery, to help them soar to new levels of personal health and growth. This is what indigenous healers often refer to as *jungle medicine* or *sacred magic*.

From our unforgotten indigenous memory, when we minister to patients at the soul level, dramatic healings often occur—sudden remissions, quite unlike the step-by-step, stop-and-start progress made in fifty-minute weekly sessions. Create an overarching ceremony, include some thoughtfully crafted rituals, marinate someone in a sacred, outdoor setting, add a measure of placebo and the company of a loving community, all the while tapping into the patient's belief system and suggestibility, and you have a recipe that can eliminate almost any physical or psychological malady. I have repeatedly observed and experienced this "miracle" of Nature.

It wasn't until I encountered a dying man in the Ecuadorian Amazon that I was pressured to "go all in" and fully practice what I had been preaching. It was one thing to observe shamans being the choreographers of ceremonies and the carpenters of rituals, but prior to being thrust into the responsibility of caring for a dying Achuar tribesman I really had not applied my natural, soul-based approach in such a profound way. The following story is *not* intended to showcase myself as some kind of miraculous healer; rather, it is my intent to highlight the *super natural* healing potential that all of us can tap. Whether as healers or patients, there is an archetypal gift that is carried forward from one ancestor to another, a storehouse of inner-healing instincts that has never been lost. Nor has it died; it is only forgotten when it is not practiced and when these artful gifts are allowed to atrophy. We simply have to put down our electronic gadgetry, quiet our world, and listen for the inner guidance that arises from countless generations of quiescent ancestral teachings, relatives who inherited this way of knowing and healed in this natural way—in what is truly *best practice.*

Jungle Medicine

The Amazon jungle of Ecuador, especially during the rainy season, can pose challenges of comfort and health for some of the most intrepid travelers. The torrential rains seemingly come from multiple directions all at once. Quickly water can build up in what was, just moments before, a large open space. Rivulets suddenly form where no water was previously present; they become streams, and worms the size of small snakes begin to slither by your feet.

There are the ever-present reminders of lurking jaguars and giant anacondas, as well as the frequently encountered tarantulas. No matter what precautions you take, chiggers and fire ants easily find their way en masse into your tent and sleeping bag and eventually invade your underwear. The welts and resultant itching can last for days, if not weeks—an enduring souvenir of the Amazon. Pesky mosquitos add to the jungle ambiance, reminding you that malaria may be part of the travel bargain. And then there are the wasp nests that, should you bump into them, can unleash a squadron of stinging avengers who can cause your body to swell up to the point that you are no longer recognizable, even to friends.

Where I go there are no outdoor latrines; nor is there running water to help remove the caked-on dirt. There are just the muddy, piranha-filled rivers and tributaries in which to "clean" yourself. And towels? Well, they never fully dry, even after having been strung from a rope for days under a thatched shelter. Dampness and unpleasant odor become your constant companions. Under these circumstances, food preparation includes abundant bacterial risks, as our sanitized and unacclimated bodies quickly tell us, the first sign of which is usually dysentery, often accompanied by infection, fever, and vomiting.

Amazingly, many people get used to most of the hazards, inconveniences, and perils over the course of a few days. Being around the calming influence of well-adjusted indigenous people can be very reassuring. Noting that *they* can be content in the rainforest, an outsider can quickly follow suit.

The Achuar

I traveled to Ecuador's southwestern region to visit one small and isolated Achuar community. Largely untouched by tourism, this particular community has been impacted by encroaching international oil companies, lumber operations, and government politicians lurking with unceasing promises of a better life if tribes commit their allegiance. There are also the mysterious and unsolved murders of the few remaining shamans residing in the Ecuadorian and Peruvian borderland. For these reasons, I am withholding the exact name and location of this Achuar tribe. They appreciate their solitude and the safety it provides.

Truth be told, the Achuar are content subsisting in the rainforest that is, in every practical and real sense, regarded as a benevolent part of their extended family. The jungle is not experienced as a brutal or particularly difficult environment. It is very much like a human relative that supports its inhabitants; there is a mutually beneficial reciprocity. The Achuar are satisfied living without currency, taxes, electricity, toilets, medical clinics, cell phones, computers, churches, psychologists, and police officers. Their simple daily needs are reliably met by the rich ecosystem and *Nunkui,* their name for God. Nunkui is an animistic deity, thought to be the life breath that emanates from the rainforest. The Achuar believe that Nunkui gives them the oxygen they breathe and is the lungs for every inhabitant.

I traveled with two interpreters, one who speaks Achuar and is also fluent in Spanish, the other my personal guide, Julian, who speaks Spanish and English. An American psychologist from Massachusetts, Steven, completed the group. Our tiny Cessna landed on a mud strip carved out of the jungle. Achuar children, upon hearing the approaching buzz of our plane, scrambled out of the forest to witness the arrival of their exotic-looking guests. The community president (similar to a chief), Ernesto, came into the clearing and forcefully blew into a clay-baked horn that announced our arrival and our numbers, and summoned the community to come forward to greet us.

Soon women appeared carrying buckets of *chicha*, an alcoholic beer made from manioc (cassava) roots mixed with river water and brewed in the sun for a few weeks. Women chew the roots to pulverize them, spitting the resulting product and its residual juices into buckets. Their saliva contains an enzyme that activates the fermenting process. In this way, chicha literally circulates from mouth to mouth.

The women, with their eyes averted to the side to avoid the displeasure of their male partners, quietly approached us and filled earthenware bowls filled with the sour and cloudy brew for us to enjoy. I understood that to decline such a gift would be quite an insult. So, we imbibed, albeit warily and without much enthusiasm. My sips were regular but small, designed to impart a sense of enjoyment. Once the women noted that the beer was disappearing, they immediately filled the bowls to the top again. With a swipe of their fingers across the lip of the bowl, they "cleansed" the area we drank from while chasing flies away. When the brew was finished, the bowls were tipped upside down and placed on a wooden rack, where they were exposed to all kinds of creatures before being used again.

Chicha can constitute as much as 80 percent of the Achuar diet for everyone—men, women, and children alike. No one ever appeared to be intoxicated, as the structured and ceremonial ingestion of the brew provided social regulation. Addiction is not an issue for them.

The Shaman Appears

Eventually a wooden chair was placed in a central commons area beneath a thatched canopy. It was designated for the region-ally renowned shaman, Rafael. Surrounding benches were assembled, providing seating for everyone else. We drank more chicha until Rafael arrived. He was wearing a colorful cloth lower wrap, a contemporary-style, buttoned white shirt, criss-crossed beads hanging from his neck, and a headdress festooned with red and yellow feathers. His cheeks, nose, and chin were painted with black, horizontal paint lines, creating a menacing look. Always remaining expressionless, he verbally sparred in rhythmic ceremonial style with another tribesman, as if to create the appearance of a heated, nonstop debate between the two men, each talking over the other as if trying to have the last word. It was a feigned argument, a form of entertainment for

FIGURE 4. Achuar Shaman Rafael. He preferred to sit twenty feet apart with a rifle always resting on his legs. (Author's photograph)

their visitors from afar. Their physical posture resembled the face-to-face throat singing I have witnessed among Inuit women and, similarly, was a prideful presentation.

The Achuar have a legendary reputation for being one of the area's warring tribes. Legend has it that they engaged in head-shrinking of enemies, but there is little if any information to support that notion. Their violent nature has been somewhat exaggerated. Long thought to be a fearsome people, they seem to have maintained this reputation, perhaps because of their ominous, black facial paintings—like the ones Rafael was wearing now—and the periodic brandishing of firearms.

So, this was my first notion of Rafael, the region's most praised shaman, who is referred to as a *juunt,* a great man. I had sought him out because he was one of the very few remaining shamans in the area who held rare healing information and talents.

Rafael and his three wives live in a large but otherwise typical Achuar home, oval in shape with semiopen palm walls, strung with hammocks and covered by a thatched roof. Upon being invited into his home for conversation, I was instructed to respect Rafael's boundaries, sitting fifteen to twenty feet away from him in the front room while a rifle rested continuously across his legs. Never did I find Rafael threatening, however; quite the reverse was true. Being that I was an outsider and a complete stranger, and considering prior dangerous experiences with white invaders, Rafael had to be on guard for any potential nefarious behavior on my part. To maintain the peace, I was cautioned by my Achuar guide not to look directly at his wives; to do so could be perceived as a threat.

This was my preferred style of anthropological travel, something I looked forward to in part as a reprieve from more trying personal and professional relationships in the States. Many people would regard this type of adventure as unappealing, even potentially traumatic. Yet, I have repeatedly found great appeal in being in the company of authentic indigenous people with their comparatively undefended personalities and lifestyles that are closely connected to the life-sustaining Mother referred to throughout South America as *Pachamama*.

The Sacred Waterfall

Julian informed Rafael that I was a healer, somewhat like him. He seemed to size me up, more by my demeanor than by any of my words that were being translated. Based on Rafael's affirming response, I believe Julian may have embellished my reputation. Because Achuar shamans continuously want to augment their healing powers, Rafael suggested I accompany him downriver in a hand-hewn canoe and hike through the jungle to a sacred waterfall. That was where ancestors were said to congregate, along with power animals such as anaconda and jaguar. Rafael decided we would go to the falls and receive their powers and strengthen ourselves. The torrential downpour that then began in no way altered the plans. In fact, with more water flowing over the falls, greater healing power would be bestowed, Rafael explained. So, we departed, first by canoe and then by foot, at the height of the storm and flooding.

After an hour of tramping through the dimly lit and wet jungle in knee-high rubber boots, I was totally drenched by the rain and repeatedly slipped into the oozing flow of mud. Sometimes the suction underfoot was so strong that it was difficult to extract my feet, boots still intact, to be able to take the next step forward. Eventually I heard the encouraging sound of rushing water, suggesting that we were getting close to the falls. Because of my slow pace, I became separated from Rafael and was alone when I arrived at the bank of a once small but now flooding river. I was at the crest of the waterfall yet unable to see the pool below. I concluded that Rafael had forded the powerful current without difficulty, so I should be able to do the same. Knowing that less than a foot of rapidly flowing water can sweep cars from a roadway, I realized that crossing the much deeper river was going to be treacherous. I leaned into the current, assuming that if its power swept me away, at least I would be washed over the falls, feet first. With a staff in hand to brace myself, I gingerly reached the opposite shore, from where I could see Rafael standing under the wash below, stripped of most of his clothing and mixing some sort of concoction in a cup. I descended an apparent trail to join him.

I followed his lead and undressed. Rafael approached me with a cup that was filled with a mixture of dark tobacco, his saliva, and rainwater. I recognized that he had prepared some *nicotiana rustica*, a wild tobacco known as *mapacho* in South America. From other experiences in South America as well as in Africa, I knew that wild tobaccos were far, far more powerful sources of nicotine than American cigarettes. Among indigenous cultures, this kind of tobacco is used for a variety of purposes. It protects and enhances shamanic healing energy, cleanses the body, provides mental clarity, and very importantly, stimulates dream activity. Tilting my head back, Raphael poured a small amount into one nostril at a time, indicating I should snort it. The juice entered my nasal cavities, and I could feel it burning its way inward. And then some of the overflow was swallowed and joined the chicha that I had ingested earlier.

We respectfully greeted and propitiated the ancestors and power animals. Then we waded across a pool to position ourselves directly under the funneled force coming from above, staggering to stay upright on slippery rocks, hoping no tree branches would come crashing down upon us. We raised our arms and gazed into the flow while entreating the ancestral and animal spirits to provide us with guidance and power. I felt cleansed, comfortable, even serene. After the short ceremony, we returned to camp.

An Achuar Dream Circle

That evening, I was encouraged to retire early, as we would be awakened by 4:00 a.m. the following morning, long before sunrise. We had been invited to Ernesto's home, where we would sit in a circle with his family, children included, and participate in another type of cleansing ceremony. The Achuar, like most indigenous cultures, is a dream society. Each morning they are encouraged to arise before the sun comes up and purge themselves, emptying themselves of anything negative from the day before, after which they recount the dreams of the previous night. Then they are off to a fresh start under the guidance of their dreams.

Upon awakening, we started walking in the dark jungle, headlamps lighting the path, headed toward Ernesto's hut. Steven and I scoured our memories for any traces of dreams. Customarily, if I don't retrieve part of a dream experience immediately upon awakening, I have little chance of retaining it and may not become aware of its details or veiled messages. Initially that day, I concluded that I had no dreams to share, but suddenly and unexpectedly clear and powerful details of a dream suddenly reemerged.

"Oh my God," I exclaimed. "Oh my God!"

Before sharing details of my dream, first I had to cleanse myself. Along with my companions, I ingested copious amounts of highly caffeinated *guayusa* tea until I couldn't force any more of it down. That was by ritual design. As a result, all of us emptied the contents of our stomachs onto the jungle's floor. There was a steady cacophony of group vomiting.

Sitting by a fire just outside Ernesto's hut, we were swarmed by insects and the huge vampire bats that follow them, swooping close to our heads. Ernesto inquired if anyone had a dream to share. I was the only one to respond, so all attention was focused on what I was about to say. I recalled being in an old home of mine in Minnesota, situated in a forested area. Visiting family members were milling about in the living room when noises were detected from a rear area of the house. I went to inquire and discovered my now-deceased father, who, because of his Parkinson's, had been unable to walk before his death. But in the dream, there he was, weakly staggering forward in an effort to join us. He was completely soaked in water and seemed determined to walk under his own power. I glanced about the room at the rest of the family, and tacitly we agreed not to offer any assistance that could detract from his gallant effort and spoil the moment. Collectively, everyone seemed to know that if any of us provided a helping hand it would hurt his pride and interfere with his sense of personal accomplishment. Then abruptly Father's pants, heavy from the water, slid down. Again, we said and did nothing, acting as if we didn't notice, while he struggled to pull the pants up on his own, regaining his dignity.

From the rear of the house from where Father had emerged, I could detect the sound of water sloshing around. I investigated and discovered a pool of water extending outdoors from what had once been my son's bedroom. Fish were swimming in the water. Arising from the water was a white bear, not an albino or a polar bear, but what aboriginal people such as the T'simshian of British Columbia call the *Kermode*, or "Spirit Bear." It is a unique member of the black bear family that is believed to hold extraordinary healing power. I noted a faint brown spot below its neck, but otherwise, it was silky white. Recognizing Spirit Bear, I fell to my knees, my arms outstretched, and we gently and affectionately greeted each other.

The Achuar believe that there are three types of dreams: neutral, negative/warning, and positive. The dream I had recounted was, in the minds of everyone present, a very meaningful and positive one. The group easily determined that my visit to the waterfall had been empowering, that spirits of the ancestors and power animals had bestowed their customary gifts on me. With these gifts came an obligation to use their powers for good. Furthermore, it was jointly concluded, my father had clearly been the beneficiary of a healing, as evidenced by his engagement with the sacred Spirit Bear and his regaining the ability to walk. The discussion led me to understand—in line with the perspective of many water-spirits healers—how Spirit Bear, as well as healing water, worked together to restore him. While Father may have once scoffed at indigenous medical practices as being superstitious and unfounded, his actions in the dream showed a surprising willingness to explore their curative powers, perhaps evincing a faith for which I had never given him adequate credit. In my dream it felt as if he were endorsing my ways, approving of his son.

The Plight Of Juan Fidel

When details of my dream reached Rafael, he decided that I should be consulted regarding a challenging patient who had been transported to him by canoe just days before. The patient was a man from a neighboring Achuar band by the name of Juan Fidel, and he was not responding to the shaman's best attempts to treat him. Juan was becoming despondent; his pain seemed unbearable, and his strength was rapidly failing.

Rafael, somewhat casually, said, "You will heal him today."

The assignment was made, and there would be no argument with the revered shaman.

I found Juan prostrate on a wooden, latticed bed, completely devoid of energy and vitality, his breathing extremely shallow and rattling. His most outstanding symptom was pain and pressure in his head. It had continued to increase since he had fallen in his canoe a week earlier. Apparently, he had been struck by an overhanging branch in the river that flung him forward, slamming his head sharply against a wooden seat. While he had never lost consciousness, the injury was obviously severe. Pressure continued to build within his brain every passing day. His symptoms—Steven, Julian, and I concluded—were indicative of a serious, closed-head trauma, with significant swelling of the brain being likely. Additionally, Juan complained of being unable to urinate or defecate for days; it created too much pressure and pain in his head. As a result, he was forced to discontinue eating and drinking. He had given up hope of recovery and resigned himself to dying amid strangers far from his blood family.

At first, I believed Juan might slip into a coma or even die unless we could arrange a flight out of the jungle to a modern hospital where he could be diagnosed with brain scans and treated with modern medicines. Perhaps surgery could be employed to reduce the pressure. There was, however, no radio communication available in this region of the Amazon, and no flight was scheduled to retrieve us for days, largely dependent on weather conditions. Rafael sternly admonished me for such thoughts, declaring that if Juan was flown to a hospital it would certainly lead to his demise. The very thought of leaving the Amazon could arouse more fear and perhaps kill him. Removing Juan from the rainforest in itself—which for him is life enhancing and a very real part of his extended family—could leave him feeling isolated and suppress his inner healer. Clearly, hospitalization was not an option. Curiously, my Western indoctrination was so powerful that my first inclination was to apply my culture's treatment methodologies, not Achuar ways of knowing and healing. Somewhat surprisingly, although I had written extensively about indigenous beliefs, healing ceremonies, and their amazing success, my mind didn't go there at first, even though I was in the Amazon and in the company of a shaman. Growing impatient, Rafael advised me to get to work, and he walked away as if disinterested in any further conversation. Responsibility for Juan's life was now in my hands.

Intimidated by the situation in which I found myself embroiled, I had to shift gears promptly and, for guidance, fell back on fundamental tenets of shamanic healing. I recalled my previous observations of indigenous healings, even articles I had written, which reminded me that one of the first goals of a shaman is to remove any obstacles to healing. That included my fear as well as the fear and despair Juan felt in being disconnected from the encouraging love of his family. I also reflected on the importance of assembling a healing community to potentiate his restorative process.

In addition, I noticed fear emanating from the people at Rafael's healing hut, as well as serious doubt about my professionalism expressed by my friend Steven. Emotional adjustments had to be made in our immediate environment; otherwise, the fear could become contagious and further impede Juan's health. I felt it was necessary to elevate the energy—to create a lighter vibration. This required an immediate and palpable shift to calm everyone, while raising hope and optimism. With that in mind, I encircled Juan with people of varying ages and instructed them to wear gentle smiles, continuously envisioning him in a pain-free and fully recovered state. Everyone was asked to imagine Juan standing again soon, in fact walking vigorously, and doing so with a smile on his face. I asked Juan who, among his immediate family, had the biggest smile of all, and he immediately said it was his eldest son. Given that, I said his task was to imagine and hold the look of relief and joy on his son's face once his health was restored and news reached his home. Among the present circle of supporters, I asked that there be no desperate pleading prayers or petitions, just positive thoughts. To create additional hope and strengthen the anticipation of recovery, collectively we shared our gratitude for the healing that was about to occur. The stage was now set.

While affectionate touch and extended eye contact between men had not been evinced in my short time with this Achuar group, intuition led me to ask that Juan be lifted from his bed and placed on a chair facing me, so that we could be touching each other knee to knee. With my fingers, I invited him to raise his gaze to meet my eyes, wanting Juan to see and feel the loving and supportive spirit that was enveloping me. Juan, in uncustomary fashion among his people, reached out and grasped my hands, squeezing firmly, revealing his panic and sending a silent plea for help from the mysterious white stranger sitting before him. I was one of his last remaining agents of change, the organizer of a healing ceremony that had commenced at the waterfall, as he had been told by Rafael. My intention was to lift him up emotionally to the point that inner healing forces could be activated. I shared a warm, unruffled, and reassuring smile.

Through my interpreter, Juan asked if I had any medicine from the States with me. To raise his spirit and further increase expectations, I instantly commanded Steven to rush back to my tent and return with my backpack. He quickly retrieved it and dropped the backpack at my feet. I began digging inside for a "wonder drug." Juan was told that I was searching for medicines that might help him. Sure enough, I found the appropriate "medications," which included nothing more than a vitamin C tablet and a CoQ10 antioxidant capsule. Looking relieved and encouraged, I was buttressing Juan's personal beliefs regarding the power of Western medicine and attempting to activate his placebo response. That approach, often mixed with a little sleight-of-hand, is a common practice among shamans almost everywhere. I encouraged him to wash the "medicine" down with chicha. Then I counseled Juan to be patient, saying it may be many minutes, or longer, before he would begin to feel relief. In this way, he was given time to imagine and anticipate reprieve from the severe pain.

Next, I leaned forward and pulled his shoulders toward me. Our foreheads met, and I generated bodily paroxysms—vibrations in my body that he could see and feel. Shifting his internal energy in this way, we stayed together for a minute or so, convulsing as one. I chanted whatever positive words that immediately came to my mind. From the Ojibwa people of northern Manitoba, I began reciting what few Anishinaabe words I was familiar with, words that summon us to go inward to our own hearts where healing originates. To change his vibration further, I guided Juan into mimicking my speech, slowly increasing our combined volume, which implied growing strength and power. The addition of mystery in the form of shaking, chanting, and incantations was intended to invoke *sacred magic,* opening his mind to previously unforeseen outcomes. Then I asked Juan to match his breathing rhythmically with mine—slowly at first, then increasing in speed and depth. I was also hoping that our physical closeness might allow for heart entrainment, so that he could absorb some of the calm I was feeling.

After about forty minutes, when Juan was appearing to regain some strength, I encouraged him to stand up with me. Apparently emboldened by the rituals and a radical shift in perspective, he was able to do so. I walked him out from the shade of the hut and into the sunlight. Standing behind him while grasping his wrists, together we raised our arms skyward, expressing thanks to Nunkui for the healing that has just transpired. In doing so, I wanted to cement the notion of a completed healing in his mind. And with that pronouncement, the first of several smiles graced his face. Hope had overtaken fear! A shift in energy—a new field—appeared to emerge, something very palpable. Juan began socializing for the first time since his arrival: more good medicine. But was he still in grave danger? I wondered.

A Final Extraction Procedure And Goodbyes

Later that afternoon, Rafael suggested that I assist him in cutting and preparing *ayahuasca* vines for another ritual that would conclude Juan's healing ceremony. Ayahuasca is an entheogen that is often confused with psychedelics. The word *entheogen* comes from a Greek root that means "to realize the Divine within." And entheogens, like ayahuasca, are plant-spirit medicines that awaken or generate mystical experiences, transporting persons to altered states in which a health reset can occur. This would be a familiar treatment for Juan and all Achuar, one that would be administered in the dark of night.

After Rafael and I had ingested some of the brew ourselves and, as a result, shared the same internal healing consciousness, we came together for an extraction ritual. Juan drank a small dose of the extraordinarily bitter brew. And with Juan laying on a wooden bench, Rafael mysteriously installed healing *tsentsak*—what are regarded as ethereal, magic healing darts or healing creatures used in shamanic practices throughout much of the rainforest. Then sucking and spitting could be heard as the causes of Juan's illness were removed from his body and discarded. Rafael has very thick phlegm, which shamans prefer. With it he is better able to capture the causes of illness and spit them out before swallowing them. Deposited on the Earth Mother, Pachamama, this cast-off material is transformed back into life-enhancing forces in a way much like composting works. Out of illness comes health, thanks to the transformative power of the earth. In this cosmovision, nothing is completely good or bad when it comes to illness. It is primarily an informative process that calls for a reset to harmony. (For a summary of the techniques used in healing Juan, see the appendix.)

I fell asleep that night with pleasant reflections of the day distracting me from the ever-present fire ants. I was amazed by the outcome of the entire process. Much later, but in the jungle darkness well before dawn, I nervously awakened to sounds outside my mesh-net tent. Opening my eyes, I discovered another person's face looking at me, just inches away and speaking in the Achuar language. I felt uneasy and confused. Julian was also awakened by the disturbance and interceded. The voice, we quickly surmised, was Juan's. He had searched for my tent in the night to announce his goodbye. Feeling healed and strong, he was planning to depart for home at sunrise, but he wanted to find me and say thank you before our group set out on any additional jungle travels. Just the day before, Juan had been suffering from what seemed to be an extremely severe and perhaps life-threatening brain injury. Now he recognized that he was well on his way to recovery and soon would be heading downriver to rejoin his family. Restored to his usual state of harmony, he now had rapidly improving internal conditions that would continue to foster health. Fear was gone; gratitude and hope replaced it.

Hours later, the sky brightened, and the customary heavy clouds dispersed. I detected the distant sound of an approaching airplane. With a break in the long rains, this was our opportunity to move on. Our pilot, hundreds of miles away, had seen a break in the weather on radar and determined that this would be a good time to extricate us from the jungle. As soon as the plane landed, we quickly hoisted our belongings onboard, much of them covered in mud. Wasting no time in this short window of opportunity to depart, we taxied to the end of the earthen runway readying for takeoff. At the very last moment, Juan stepped out of the jungle to the side of the runway, smiling and waving with gratitude.

Additional Mysteries

Once we reached the Puyo airport at the edge of the jungle, and after being out of connection with the outside world for several days, Julian turned on his smartphone to reconnect with his normal world. Upon reading a surprising email from a friend with whom he had long ago fallen out of touch, he appeared mystified and frozen. He didn't speak for what seemed like an interminable amount of time. It felt as though he had just received some bad news.

I silently and patiently waited for a clue about what was happening. Finally, Julian broke the silence. The email message described how his old friend had just learned of a unique animal that he had never heard of before and felt sure would interest Julian. It was the Canadian Spirit Bear from the far north. *How could this be?* Julian wondered. Attached was a photo of the beautiful, white animal, befittingly with a slight brown spot just below her neck, *exactly* as the bear had appeared in my dream! We didn't have words for that moment, just quiet reflection of the mysteries that abound.

One might think that that would be the end of an amazing story. There were, however, additional and poignant concluding pieces.

Six months later, I returned to the same area of the Amazon with Julian. Of course, Juan remained on my mind, and I wondered how he was doing. I thought I'd check on him. After canoeing for many hours to get within a few miles of where he was thought to live, I asked some local Achuar men if anyone knew of a man named Juan Fidel. They were familiar with the name. I went on to ask if anyone knew of his health status, and the reply I received was disturbing. They told me, "He died months ago from a head injury—a canoe accident." Crestfallen by the news, I asked Julian to request directions so that we might travel to his community and visit with his surviving family members. Feeling extremely discouraged, we set out for his home.

The distance traveled was fairly short, but the trip seemed interminably long. We beached our canoes ashore at the foot of a small hill. We scrambled to the top where there was a clearing and a few huts. Pushing through the tall grasses and stepping into the open area, there stood Juan wearing the same smile I had seen on his face when we departed many months before.

He approached me in his one and only dress shirt saying, "I had a dream last night that you were coming to check on me, so I've been waiting for you."

Without hesitation, we shared a hearty embrace, once again breaching the Achuar taboo of little male-to-male contact. My elation had to be very apparent. I gifted Juan with tobacco, and he introduced me to relatives, suggesting that perhaps I would want some photographs of his family. A photo of the two of us now adorns my home. And I have another photo on display, this one of a young, smiling Achuar girl who originally sat in Juan's healing circle. Her beautiful smile now presides over the patients who sit in my office.

Oh, the lessons we can receive while far from "civilization"! I returned from Ecuador with many memories and sentiments

FIGURE 5. Reunion with Juan Fidel. We were meeting again six months after I had treated him in the Amazon. (Author's photograph)

about the jungle: the beauty of the land and its people, awe and appreciation for the restorative power of our inner physician, and a revitalized healing spirit embedded in the mysterious recesses of my soul. But most importantly, I was gifted with the enduring friendship of the remarkable Juan Fidel. As I type these words, tears come.

Many inquiries have been made about the techniques I employed in the jungle. Ethical questions and moral dilemmas abound. What would have been the greater misjudgment—to have used placebo "medications" deceptively, as I did, or to have *not* used them and watched Juan die, playing it safe? Or should I have refused to treat him and turned that responsibility back to Rafael? Should I have waited for the weather to clear and the plane to arrive, extracting Juan from his rainforest "family" despite the protests? And if the outcome had been dramatically different—If Juan had died—how would the Achuar community and Juan's relatives have responded to me? Would their opinion affect me any more than would judgments from my licensing board?

Rafael's Health

In Rafael's community, members of the tribe can become highly antagonized when a healing goes awry and the desired outcome isn't forthcoming. Before my second visit to the area, Rafael was asked to heal the young child of a neighboring tribesman. When his efforts proved unsuccessful and the child died, the grief-stricken father hid along the shoreline in thick vegetation awaiting Rafael's coming. The father shot the shaman twice in the head as Rafael canoed downriver accompanied by one of his wives. That incident occurred just weeks after Rafael and I had traversed the same river in the same canoe. Astonishingly, Rafael was still alive and carrying on with his life when I returned a year later. The wounds did not kill him. In a not-uncommon shamanic way, Rafael successfully treated himself.

Locals have now concluded that Rafael is a far more powerful man and healer than ever before. After all, he had received no outside medical care and had healed himself, proving to all that he is impervious even to bullets. Sometimes individuals answer a calling early in their life to serve and heal. Often it follows a significant health crisis. Again and again, they can be challenged to renew their commitment, especially after life-threatening experiences are encountered and surmounted. Surviving bullets to the head is enough for most people to consider a new ministry, but in the shamanic world the response to a severe crisis is often quite different. Now, as a result of Rafael's brush with death, the community's belief in his shamanic healing powers has been greatly enhanced. Nevertheless, I know that Rafael will always keep a rifle ever ready on his lap when visitors arrive, myself included.

The Heart of Bushman
Spirituality and Healing

There are an estimated fifty thousand San Bushmen residing in Botswana, Namibia, Angola, and South Africa, of which fewer than three thousand still live as hunters and gatherers. Unfortunately, that way of life, with its supportive sense of community, its predictability, and its abundance of leisure is fast disappearing.

Many miles to the north, far from these relatively well-studied people, are the Hadza—or *Hadzabe*—Bushmen, living in the Great Rift Valley region of Tanzania. Estimates vary of the number of Hadza who remain, but it is likely less than one thousand. Some say as few as five hundred still exist. Somewhat different from their distant relatives to the southwest, this remote group of gentle and self-sustaining hunters and gatherers employ far less ritualized and detailed healing methods than do most indigenous cultures. Their religious beliefs are every bit as amorphous and fluid as those of Bushmen to the south and every bit as intriguing.

Dance and Trance Ceremonies

"Healing makes our hearts happy," say the Ju/'hoansi Bushmen of the western Kalahari. They believe that ministering to each other during community ceremonies is not only a way to heal illnesses; but just as importantly, the Giraffe Dance also holds the promise of perpetually restoring important social ties. Healing is more than about illness; it is part of the social glue that strengthens personal bonds. In this way, southern Bushman medicine is as much a preventive activity as it is a curing practice. It is about reciprocal relationships with one another, their vague gods, their revered ancestors and spirit forces, and the cosmos.

A spiritual energy naturally arising from the earth, called *num,* is at the core of many of their community healing trance dances. It can be likened to kundalini energy that rises from the feet and spreads throughout the body. Sharing num with band members (and visitors) occurs during dance and generates an altered state called *kia.* This happens through the laying on of hands and is the primary way traditional Bushmen prefer to remove illness. Because everyone carries the potential to receive num, there are no clear shamans among many Bushman groups. Everyone has healing abilities—some more pronounced than others. Many believe that women are greater conduits of this life force emanating from the earth, and frequently men look to them to "power-up" when they share the energy.

As num is activated by ceremonial singing and dancing, it begins to "boil" inside the dancers' bodies, sometimes feeling as if a burning arrow has entered their abdomens, causing them to bend forward. While num energy is eagerly pursued by most adult Bushmen, it can create both fear and physical pain. Violent spasms, wobbly legs, impaired vision, profuse sweating, and stabbing pain are all a part of the process of generating healing num. I have witnessed individuals passing out from its power, as well as hands landing in the central fire they dance around, only to come away from the experience with no pain, burns, or scarring. Something about the altered state appears to prevent harm from befalling the dancers when consumed with num. They are, in some important way, separated from this dimension.

As gut-wrenching and exhausting as the experience of generating num can be, Bushmen are eager to participate because of the many benefits it offers, whether in giving or receiving energy. Beyond the improved health and the strong sense of community, an "afterglow" of sexual-like intimacy follows the dancing. It is a sensual feeling of closeness that is usually not played out in actual sexual encounters.

Bushman energy medicine is a part of Africa's prehistory. In South Africa, I have viewed ancient cave-wall depictions that have been scientifically dated, providing evidence that the Bushmen have not significantly changed their energy-medicine practices in over sixty thousand years. The body postures of the human figures in their art repeatedly hint of a belief in ancestral contact, with the hands and gaze of the figures raised upward and a series of dots seemingly connecting them to something in the heavens above. What is uniform among these southern Bushman groups, as has been recognized over time, is not only the healing power derived from being intimately attached to the earth, but also the ongoing, felt connection to ancestors who have departed their earthly existence.

We know much about the San, !Kung, and Ju/'hoansi Bushmen and their healing methods, but far less has been written about their distant northern relatives. I set out to meet the Hadza and discovered that their culture is far less permeated by healing activities, perhaps, in part, because they appear to have far fewer health concerns. Their more limited ceremonies are designed more to maintain social cohesion than to remedy ailments.

Arrival

In the summer of 2011, I had my first of two opportunities to visit two Hadza encampments in northwest Tanzania. My original intentions were to view them through the lens of medical anthropology. Quickly I realized that this was a unique culture. The Hadza maintain a reverent and quite primal anchor to their long-familiar land. Theirs is a fluid and harmonious way of life that could, if left untouched, sustain them for thousands of years more and guide "civilized" societies.

On the initial leg of my first trip to Tanzania, a middle-aged woman from Iowa sat next to me on the plane and asked the usual perfunctory questions: "Who are you?" "Where are you from?" "Where are you going?"

I explained that I was embarking on a trip to visit the Hadza Bushmen, which prompted her half observation, half question, "So, you are a missionary?"

Without hesitation, I responded, "Yes, I am a *reverse* missionary. I travel to remote cultures and study their spiritual ideas and lifestyles, returning with observations that might edify Western society."

That was not the response she was expecting, nor the kind of response I customarily give, accurate as it may be.

The Hadza are hunter-gatherers in the strictest sense, their lifestyle virtually unchanged over thousands of years. A band's whereabouts follows the existing food supply. This requires relocating their bands of twenty to thirty people every two months or so. Consequently, they were difficult to find on my initial visit. Their ancient, wooded homeland is along a 2,000-kilometer line beginning near Lake Eyasi and extending down the Serengeti Plateau. Fortunately, I traveled with a trusted Maasai guide, Kambona Mollel, who spoke Swahili and Kiswahili, the mother tongues of his people who live in the surrounding rolling hills. His language skills were enough to forge communication with neighboring Datoga tribal herders, and with one of them driving us into the area, we had enough expertise to learn the details of the whereabouts of one Hadza group. For hours, we slowly lumbered ahead in our Land Cruiser, down first roads, then rock-strewn trails, and then barely distinguishable pathways. Eventually, after having punctured two tires and being down to the last spare, we felt surprisingly calm and speculated that we were finally in Hadza territory. Now it was time to stop, because the dense trees seemed impenetrable by vehicle.

We carefully scanned the area for smoke; perhaps a campfire was burning nearby. Nothing. Then, as if being summoned by some unknown form of communication, a man came running out of the forest toward us. He was very dark-skinned, dressed in shorts, and in a badly tattered shirt. It was a Hadza, who, we would soon learn, was assigned to monitor a camp area while other men were away hunting. He had noticed us wandering around, looking lost, and assumed we were searching for his people. He pointed to himself and said, "Kampala." We did the same to identify ourselves. And without further attempts at communication, Kampala ran toward the forest. Quickly I grabbed a backpack jammed with essentials, and Kambona and I followed him. Our driver hollered to us, saying he would stay back and do vehicle repairs.

We were guided into an opening that had six grass huts with several braided mats on the ground where women and children were enjoying a quiet day of socializing. We had found the Hadza—or, more accurately, they had found us. Appearing fully to trust their guests, they immediately invited us to sit on a mat among the women and children, with one elderly woman, perhaps in her eighties, resting about twenty yards away. Conversation commenced, and it seemed remarkably easy to gather information about this particular group. We didn't need to know their complex language, Hadzane, as Swahili provided a satisfactory bridge. As for me, I spoke with gestures alone, an attentive Kampala appearing to understand me.

Children were never more than a few feet away from their mothers or other adults. Cloth bindings kept the youngest children bound closely to their mothers, comforted by touch at all times. The adults lovingly doted on the children, and we never heard a child cry, even upon falling. Eye contact between mothers and their children was nearly constant, and the bonds of understanding and solace appeared to be very strong. Kampala, in very pragmatic terms, said it would be unwise to allow children to cry, especially at night, as their vulnerable sounds might attract a predator—perhaps a lion, leopard, or hyena.

Despite all the apparent child indulgence, though, even at a very young age children did their part to support the community. Being intimately tied to the rhythms of the adults, children as young as two, noting the unwanted incursion of Datoga cattle into camp, assisted the adults by grabbing sticks and herding them away—the giant animals responding to the direction even of tiny children! The men could easily have quietly shot the invading livestock with poisoned arrows and harvested some quick food. But the Hadza didn't give that option any serious consideration. They believe that wild animals provide the favored food, even though much effort must be expended on distant hunts. The domesticated cattle are the respected property of their neighbors; it is indigenous animals that are on the earth for the Hadza. Being conflict avoidant, the Hadza have no desire to provoke discord with a neighboring tribe.

FIGURE 6. Hadza Mother and Child Bonding. Mothers rarely lose eye contact with their children. (Author's photograph)

Health

Chronic stress is nonexistent. The Hadza are largely free of lasting trauma and seem to suffer only momentary pain. Upsets and painful events simply come and go; they are just brief interruptions on any given day. The Hadza have the ability quickly to empty their minds, reset themselves, and routinely start anew. In Western cultures, stress and illness often arise from being "here" while wanting to be "there." The Hadzas' ancient and familiar way of existing in the moment at hand allows them to feel natural, congruent, and serene and orients them to one another and to place. Even a child's death, which is not uncommon, is something they can let go of relatively quickly. It isn't that they are heartless. Quite to the contrary, they are a compassionate and nurturing society. But their habitual ease with the natural flow of life and death prevents Hadza parents from holding on to the grief of a lost child for very long. And because they don't hang on to suffering—a universal contributor to physical and emotional illnesses across most cultures—the Hadza enjoy robust health without the need for doctors, clinics, or pharmaceuticals. They have resisted persistent efforts by the Tanzanian government to impose Western medical practices and formal education on what many consider a backward group of people. And compared to other Bushmen living in southern Africa, they have escaped the pesky Christian missionaries.

The Hadza seem to be spared epidemics that neighboring cultures experience. In fact, they enjoy much better health than other rural Africans. Researchers have discovered that they have extremely good eyesight, despite being outdoors every day without sunglasses. Hadza hearing is excellent. Obesity, heart disease, and cancer are rare. Women's menstrual periods are light and short. They sleep on the bare ground, on impala hides, or in caves but do not suffer from significant bodily discomfort or arthritis. Because the Hadza enjoy vigorous health and are quite egalitarian, few individuals are needed to fill the roles of shamans or health specialists. Living in their small groups of twenty to thirty people and often roaming the land barefoot in remote areas requires every individual to be versed in healing methods. Because of this roving, hunter-gatherer lifestyle, healthcare must be a personal skill passed on to everyone by the elders and carried with them. They will forage for healing plants as needed, just as they forage for food when hungry. No medicine bag or first-aid kit is necessary. Each person—or at least someone close by—will likely have a remedy for any physical malady encountered. Healing practices are not mystical or magical in nature; they entail simple, common-sense information that everyone possesses.

Malnutrition is not an issue. The Hadza diet is more diverse than the highly monotonous rice, maize, beef, and milk diets of neighboring pastoralists such as the Maasai and Datoga. The Hadzas eat sporadically as hunger arises. A group may go for days without food, experiencing little discomfort or disconcerting hunger, and then devour substantial calories after a large kill. This is quite unlike binge eating in the West, which is intended to fill an emotional void by providing massive pleasure. Hadza eating patterns reflect a bodily rhythm akin to that of lions or leopards that eat ravenously and then rest extensively in community. Like the native animals of their land, the Hadza act entirely according to inner promptings. Unlike us, they are not bound by clock time or light for their eating habits but instead are regulated by an internal sense of what is needed and when.

Childbirth

My guide, Kambona, described how the Hadza, at least historically, had their unique way of bringing a child into this world. To guarantee a successful childbirth and ensure an infant's healthy start in life, mothers delivered their children inside the hollowed interior of a baobab tree. These giants of the forest can live as long as two thousand years and have cavernous rooms inside them. They are regarded as holy trees. A woman who was about to deliver a child would enter the chambers of a baobab with a birthing assistant. The ancient baobab would serve as the infant's second womb for four weeks and offer protection for the new life emerging inside the sacred tree. It was believed that the baobab's long lifespan was imbued on the newborn, setting the infant's life on a long and healthy course.

This is why an expectant mother would traditionally retreat to the baobab at the time of birth. Shortly thereafter, the midwife would depart to accompany the mother and child and remain with them inside the tree for the additional four weeks before returning to the community. In this private setting, not only would the tree's blessings of health be conferred upon the mother and her infant, but also a strong attachment would be formed. While in seclusion, a strong, intimate, and uninterrupted bond between the two would develop. And upon departure, the infant was swaddled to the mother, allowing the baby always to feel her reassuring presence and movement.

This is Nature's preventive medicine. Although the custom has now somewhat diminished because of the influence of the outside world, the practice of retreating to the sacred baobab tree at the time of birth remains in practice to some degree even today.

The Hadza Hunt

Usually one man, and perhaps some adolescent males, will stay back tending camp while the remaining men are off hunting. As was the case with Kampala, this leisurely time allows them to catch up on making additional arrows, fashioning arrowheads, and preparing the poison into which the projectile points will be dipped. (This poison can be made of various substances, depending on availability by season and location.) Because the poison itself is deadly to all creatures, including humans, it must be handled carefully. If it directly pierced Kampala's skin, it could kill him. He explained, however, that he knew of antidotes in Nature that could arrest the deadly process. The Hadza use tiny bows with little propulsion behind them, as the poison allows only a small force to be necessary to deliver the arrow to its target and get under the animal's hide. No matter how slight the penetration—whether to a giraffe, a gemsbok, or an eland—the fatal effect will eventually occur, even though it might require another day of tracking the wounded animal. I also learned that when the meat of a harvested animal is ingested, it is of no danger to the Hadza. The poison's potency is naturally lost, having been filtered through the body of the wild game. Hunters will even eat raw meat at the kill site immediately after the animal's death with no harm befalling them.

Kampala explained how, the evening before I met him, a hunting party had shot and wounded an impala; but darkness had descended quickly, prohibiting the *epemes* (the Hadza word for large-game hunters over the age of twenty) from tracking the animal. The following day, the hunters returned to the area and gathered the meat before hyenas, or any other scavenging animal, could claim the carcass. The epemes were expected to be back in the village within the day to share their bounty.

In circumstances when a large animal is killed, the Hadza send what my interpreter described as "wired" communications—extrasensory messages—home so that those remaining in camp can prepare neighboring bands for the sharing of any excess bounty. This prevents spoilage and waste (the Hadza do not smoke or store game) while promoting goodwill. The unique form of communication suggests that individuals still feel closely connected to one another even while, from my Western perspective, they are separated by substantial distance. Perhaps this is something akin to what Einstein referred to as "spooky action at a distance." I couldn't help concluding that the Hadza hold a conceptualization of distance that is far different and less restrictive than my own. And I wondered if their communication abilities are an ancient telepathic remnant that has disappeared in most other cultures worldwide due to a lack of use, or in part by our reliance on the written word and technology.

Sensing my eagerness to learn additional details about his culture, Kampala instructed me in the art of starting a fire without matches or flint. He put his hands over mine to direct me, and we spun a stick onto another piece of wood with fine tinder at the base. Amazingly, in less than a minute, I had started a campfire. He also allowed me to practice my aim using one of his bows as the women watched, surprised to see that I could shoot accurately. Years ago, I had enjoyed some modest success hunting with a bow. Hearing of that, Kampala suggested that I should accompany some of the younger men on a hunt the next day as they pursued smaller game, such as the dik dik (tiny deer) or the bush baby (a squirrel-size tree dweller). In anticipation,

I readied a backpack with organic granola bars, bottled water, ibuprofen, a camera, and other "essentials."

In contrast to my own preparations, in the morning adolescent boys made ready to depart with only their bows and arrows, nothing more. Food and water would assuredly be found along the way—no worries. Their torsos were cloaked with the fur hides of baboons to hide their scent and disguise themselves. We rapidly covered a lot of territory and I had difficulty keeping up, sweating profusely. The young hunters, on the other hand, moved ahead leisurely and effortlessly, following their dogs, who served as extra eyes, ears, and noses. These well-disciplined dogs never barked. They quietly went about their team duties, usually driving an animal toward the hunters or chasing small game up a tree. When a bush baby was harvested and a fire was started to prepare it, the dogs silently lay down in the background, knowing that their reward—some of the entrails—would eventually be dispensed. In a culture permeated with values of sharing and reciprocity, even the dogs trusted and respected this way of life. Everyone would be cared for.

And what would a meal be without dessert? As the small animal was being cooked, I noticed two of the teenagers watching birds flying nearby. It was explained that sometimes specific birds will indicate the location of a tree with honey inside. Indeed, that is what happened. Atop a nearby tree there was a hollow, from which bees could be seen swarming as the birds flew overhead. One hunter scaled the tree with some burning brush and filled the cavity with smoke. As some of the bees departed and others became lethargic, he reached deep into the cavity and began removing chunks of honeycomb, dropping them to those of us standing below. Bees swarmed around anyone holding a piece of honeycomb, sometimes landing on their faces, which didn't seem to alarm any of the boys. No one was stung. A chunk of this sweet treat was torn away and handed to me. Live bees were still attached to the honeycomb, and the boys bit into their portions consuming the live bees and all. I recalled a previous reaction to bee stings in the Amazon that had left me grotesquely swollen and in tremendous discomfort. Yet, here in the hills of the Serengeti, eating the insects seemed perfectly safe and life sustaining. So, I indulged, chewing and swallowing the honey-sweetened protein. Perhaps because I expected no ill effects, there were none.

Ceremony and Ritual

Compared to their southern counterparts, the northern Hadza Bushmen don't seem to hold formalized ceremonies and supportive rituals as often, although they do have celebratory hunting events. The Epeme Dance affords an opportunity to gather the community together. In these rarely documented ceremonies, the goals are to enjoy socializing as a group and to celebrate together and strengthen bonds, as well as to repair any rifts between people. This activity has rarely been seen by outsiders. It is perhaps as close to anything resembling a semiformalized religious gathering among the Hadza. The ceremony occurs after the sun has set on dark, moonless nights. If there is anything that represents a god to them, it appears to be the sun. When it sets, their more spiritual side arises.

It may seem ironic that their spirituality emerges primarily when their god, the sun, disappears, but I think it's at least, in part, a practical matter: When the day's hunting and gathering are done—in what is perhaps the equivalent of the Sabbath in some cultures—the Hadza can allow themselves the time to worship together in dance. My hunch is that when the sun retires for the evening and the black sky lights up with smaller lights—the stars—the otherworld of the gods and the ancestors seems closer to them. And they want closeness in all their relationships, everywhere. It is a time to fine tune themselves during the reflective darkness, attuning their energy to the world around them and the people with whom they are intimately connected. They dance through the night, believing that num is strongest during the waning hours just before the sun arises. And everyone wants to capture the healing and social bonding power of num at this time.

The Hadza dance I had the good fortune to witness followed the traditional pattern: Typically, only adults are in attendance; the children remain back in camp. Unlike the line-dance formation performed by other Bushman groups, in the Hadza Epeme Dance only a single man dances at a time. You could think of it as being like a karaoke party in the States; each man takes the stage by turn, with everyone united in good humor and fellowship.

The men all adorn themselves with feathers and a long dark cape. They may have jingling bells around their ankles and a gourd rattle in hand. Their dance steps will be slow, rigidly stomping on the ground one foot at a time. They may sing, shout, and whistle in the direction of the seated women, who respond with increasing fervor as the night wears on.

Eventually, the women come forward to join in the festivities and dance, too, one at a time, in the vicinity of the men. The women's style connotes feeling as well, but it is more gentle, fluid, and graceful than that of the men. The point of the dance is to bring everyone together, renew ties, and, in so doing, let go of prior disputes. The dance is also thought to bring luck in hunting.

Song and dance, characterized by repetitive melodies and rhythmic movements, are universal medicines among all traditional Bushman tribes. The Hadza also love their casual dances and are happy if you join them. Periodically they enjoy the equivalent of a line dance—what they refer to informally as a "snake dance." In these dances, they hold on to each other, not as couples do, but as an entire community in which everyone is symbolically linked. It seems obvious that this kind of Hadza "skinship" leads to kinship. Their dancing is a playful, soulful, physical, and sensuous activity, more concerned with sustaining community bonds and dissimilar from southern Bushman dance ceremonies that are primarily intended to heal. Absent from the Hadza culture, for instance, is the equivalent of the San or !Kung Bushmen's healing Giraffe Dance.

Spiritual Life

The Hadza "religion" is, simply put, their way of life. It is marked by fluidity and ambiguity, as flexible as daily living. Like that of traditional Native Americans, their sense of interconnectedness permeates all aspects of their existence and is not separate from routine activities. It is experiential, not just an exercise of the mind. It is always alive and not demarcated from everyday events or relegated to periodic ceremonies. The Hadza have no interest in knowing whether it is Sunday or a special day. Their beliefs are not fixed and, therefore, are somewhat challenging for an outsider to appreciate. No rigid dogma ties them down or severely constricts them. There is room for much individuality in this very communal society.

I was reminded of His Holiness the Dalai Lama who, when asked what religion he practiced, responded by saying, "My religion is kindness." So it is with the Hadza. Each day they wear their religion of kindness, tolerance, teamwork, generosity, patience, equality, reciprocity, suppleness, peacefulness, simplicity, playfulness, and humor. It is practiced without creeds, without books, pastors, intermediaries, or sermonizing. It needs no defining or extensive elaboration; it is just lived.

It seems that all indigenous people who have similar unbroken ties with the land they call home are blessed with this kind of spirituality; they enjoy a comfort with mystery and fluidity that modern cultures may rarely know. Hadza spirituality arises from being firmly planted on the earth—feeling its healing energy and not being shielded from Nature by technology, insulated shoes, or "protective" homes. After all, the Hadza *are* Nature.

The Hadza seem to live in a Zen-like present awareness and find complete comfort in doing so. They are satisfied living in the unhurried and leisurely moment, even when no water or food is immediately available. Time just doesn't matter; it is cyclical, not linear. If you ask them how old they are, as I did, you may get their best guess, which could be off by twenty years or more. Ask when they sleep and their rejoinder will be, "Whenever we are tired, mostly at night."

The Hadza do not store food for a proverbial "rainy day"— an idea that is foreign to them. They have such a strong sense of personal efficacy that fear does not set in when food is absent. Rather, they are adept at going for extended periods of time without food. No desperation is evident during brief periods of momentary shortage or hunger. They know how to live off the land and find food and water; and in-between hunts they socialize, sitting for hours around the campfire telling stories. When hunger arises, the men simply say to each other, "Let's go hunting tomorrow; that would be enjoyable."

Perhaps what promotes such gentleness is that they are hunters and gatherers living a communal lifestyle, with no interest in interpersonal competition, minimal fears, and only momentary stressors. They believe their collective abilities will adequately provide for them. They trust in the earth's bounty, and each group lives by an internal rhythm that is intertwined with the external rhythms of the physical world.

When life presents major challenges, they may seek guidance from deceased ancestors. Occasionally this requires a visit to burial sites atop the hills, where people will solicit advice from an elder who has recently passed over. Even in relationships with the deceased, ongoing respect and reciprocal obligations remain. It is the Hadza practice, for instance, to prepare the once-favorite meal of the departed (often eland or gemsbok) and deliver it to the burial location before asking for anything in return. Reciprocity pervades all aspects of their existence.

Aggression

The Hadza way of life is by no means perfect, and I don't want to romanticize them in an unrealistic way. They, too, experience animosity, hostility, and violence. There is even the rare murder, which is almost always tied to infidelity disputes between men over women. But overall, their society is markedly devoid of suspicion, aggression, competition, and wanting. Warfare with neighboring tribes, as with the other Bushmen, is almost nonexistent.

The pacifism of the Hadza endures despite many forms of provocations, including racism. (Their very name, *Bushmen*, is regarded in the larger African society as a racist obscenity, like the use of the *n*_____ word in U.S. history.) When neighboring tribes indifferently allow their cattle to intrude into Hadza territory, the cattle are shushed away; and, should that prove ineffective, Hadza bands are inclined to gather their sparse belongings and move on to a new, undisturbed location. They will go to great lengths to stifle aggressive impulses. If a serious argument breaks out between two people, other members of the band may move in and use raucous humor to shift emotions. Quite often, the combatants are disarmed by this approach and end up laughing together around the campfire later that day.

Hadza are happy with what they *have* and don't obsess on what they might *want*. The accumulation of possessions other than bare necessities is very limited. Beyond bows, arrows, an axe or two, a few vessels, the clothes on their backs, and some limited personal adornments, they desire nothing more. The result is a culture without intertribal rivalry, theft, raids, a desire to conquer other groups, or the dangers of accumulating wealth. Their prosperity is measured in terms of friendships, not possessions. Hadza currency is measured in their social relationships.

Laugh and be Heartsoft!

Sitting around a campfire with Hadza tribesmen, one notices how conversation is routinely interspersed with laughter. The Hadza are a lighthearted people. Mothers stare into the eyes of their infant children while bound belly to belly with a swaddling cloth, their shared smiles and mirror neurons socially binding them. Loving touch is the Hadza medicine; it softens the heart, preventing or treating all human maladies. They are love doctors. The rest of the world is seen as dehydrated by a shortage of touch.

From north to south, all traditional Bushman peoples seem to convey a similar guiding message: stay connected to each other, be *heartsoft* with all living beings, and pay attention to your feelings and spiritual energy. Anthropologist Bradford Keeney, in his book *The Bushman Way of Tracking God*, cautioned, "Holding in your spiritual energy, light, and inner gifts will give you spiritual constipation."[1] To love, support, heal, encourage, and forgive each other as the Bushmen routinely do is what Native Americans term "good medicine" or what Keeney would describe as the "awakened heart."[2] Calling the African Bushmen the "Sufis of the Kalahari," he says that they have chosen love over law, humility over hierarchy, and humor over hell, observing that this way of being has worked well for over forty-thousand years.[3] In essence, it is their best practice, their evidence-based way of healthy living.

Because the Bushmen's spiritual life has likely kept them physically healthy and smiling for thousands of years, I believe we must open our minds to the lessons of their simple, elegant, and life-affirming ways. In some of the oldest cultures on the planet, I have observed that the more people embrace uncertainty and mystery—the more they are comfortable with a Buddhist-like, *not-knowing mind*, live close to the earth, and live in the present—the closer they come to discovering a private, inner god, a familiar source of divine guidance and ordering wisdom. Whether it is in the far north of Canada, the jungles of Nicaragua or Peru, or a Hadza encampment, what my Maasai guide succinctly stated upon my departure from the Bushmen is profoundly true: "The old is gold."

A Primal Homecoming

In the ebb and flow of human development, current trends are distancing us from basic instincts, perceptive skills, and the very planet that spawned our lives. Burgeoning technologies that can think for us, pharmaceuticals that alter how we feel, and indoor creature comforts that confine us have disconnected us from our past and from Mother Earth. This so-called progress, I contend, has actually given rise to a temporary form of devolution.

As a result, there is an emotional disquiet, at least in the West, that furtively harkens us back to a partially forgotten time preceding our break with the land. While conscious thoughts and feelings can be governed by technological and media-driven distractions as well as the pills we swallow, there remains an ancient wisdom that cannot be stilled. It is a primal knowing that is indelibly imprinted in our physical being and in a vague but distant unconscious memory that refuses, by the will of Nature, to be extinguished.

In Western society, there is an overvaluation of the conscious, analytical mind and, with it, an atrophy of dozens of senses and abilities. Sojourns to the Amazon and the Serengeti have reminded me of the many skills that indigenous people have not forgotten—abilities that guide them safely through life's inevitable challenges. I have met shamans who can look into another person's body with their mind's eye to diagnosis an illness, Hadza Bushmen who can "wire" messages long distances without the use of a cell phone or a letter, and Native Americans who can smell approaching changes in the weather. It is in the quiet of Nature that shamans can listen with their hearts, skin, eyes, and noses as well as their ears—a synesthetic talent that today is largely disbelieved or simply unknown outside of indigenous cultures.

Traditional healers consciously merge with the people they are charged with healing. This can be a tedious and time-consuming process. Meanwhile, Western doctors and psychologists search for the newest scientific discoveries—innovative gadgets and apps, as well as the latest drugs—expeditiously to think and diagnose for us. All of this transpires while a treasure trove of untapped wisdom remains quiescent within us, awaiting *re*discovery.

Urbanization and technological "advances" have partially, but only temporarily, severed awareness of our deepest biological roots. The result has been a psychological and spiritual unease. Yet, an instinctual yearning for a return to Mother Earth tenaciously tugs at us. We subconsciously detect an attraction, a primal hankering, resulting from the deep grooves in our psyche etched over millions of years of human development while standing, sleeping, and healing on Mother. Our species longs for the ancient connections that we once enjoyed. This urge is the enduring remnant of a "racial memory" concealed for now in our collective unconscious. It remains very much alive in a few remote and reclusive cultures, such as the Hadza

Bushmen of Tanzania or the Mayoruna of the Amazon Basin. Just as importantly, current observation of these hunter-gatherer cultures reveals that we as individuals are not as separate as we think we are. By personally exploring and experiencing the beliefs and lifestyles of indigenous people and by returning to Nature on a routine basis—simply sitting on Mother Earth—we may be able to revive the faint feeling of our ancient, shared humanity as well as our primal connection to all animals.

The Two-Million-Year-Old Man

The past is here and now. I am referring to a storehouse of knowledge held in the body, below conscious levels, seeking expression when our minds are troubled by contemporary stressors, producing a vague but all-pervasive sense of angst. The archaic man— "the two-million-year-old Self," as Jung described him—resides at subterranean levels of the psyche. When our lives depart too far from our original patterns of survival, this old man's compass instigates a course correction. That is what is happening today in many parts of the Western world.

Our lives being nurtured in the embrace of Nature, the current disconnect can't, in a mere hundreds of years, erase our ancient inner knowing. Vague remembrances live on in our primordial soul and persistently seek expression, much like bubbles of air rising from the depths of a pond are compelled by unseen forces to surface. The resurgence of interest in indigenous wisdom and shamanic healing practices are two ways in which this ancient part of our being is now seeking expression. Spiritual tourism can be another circuitous route home. Even fishing and hunting restore this tie to a world removed from the office, away from the computer and artificial light, and free of noise, noise, noise.

Psychoanalyst Anthony Stevens, who was profoundly influenced by Jung, wrote about the collective history of our species, explaining how it is biologically encoded in human consciousness. The code owes its existence to origins that are long forgotten at the cognitive level but still guide us, although mysteriously shrouded in the primordial mists of evolutionary time. We can think of this collective history as defined by *archetypes*—unconsciously organized ideas and images inherited from our earliest ancestors.

Today's spiritual and psychological meanderings reflect longstanding and basic human needs. To assuage our angst, we in Western culture appear to be seeking a consoling relationship with Nature—the ultimate Mother—or, as the Lakota would say, the Big Holy. Another way of envisioning our current angst is to apply the psychological term, *attachment disorder.* When a comforting or life-sustaining bond with the parent is abruptly severed, children instinctively set out in search of a substitute calming force. They may move from person to person, relationship to relationship, only to experience a series of unrewarding, *insecure attachments*. In adulthood, the suffering may be expressed as a drug dependency, a sexual addiction, or an eating disorder as the now-grown children try to fill their emptiness with momentary pleasures and excitement—their new "best friends." But always the search is for the original source of security and nurturance, for the natural, human mother who disappeared from their lives. We modern humans, in our technology-driven lives, can be said to be suffering the same attachment disorder on a collective level in our separation from Mother Earth. Considering the entire span of human evolution, this sense of detachment from Nature has been sudden and traumatic—taking place a mere two hundred years ago or so. It was then that we really stepped off the land, entered our physical structures, and went outside less and less. That is when our soul went adrift.

Nature as Library and Sanctuary

Nature is a sanctuary for the human soul. The wilderness can heal the soul if we are willing to visit her. Wild places are permeated with a maternal understanding of our species' relationships with all life forms. Our bodies and minds are sustained by the elemental forces of Nature. And she is a library, as Luther Standing Bear said, with knowledge inherent in all things including wind, stones, leaves, grass, streams, birds, and animals—every life form can be regarded as a teacher. Some of Nature's tonic comes to us when we settle into her ancient rhythms. As the mind becomes uncluttered in wilderness settings, with its loud silence, Nature consoles and refuels our primitive spirit. Being outdoors and directly on the land fosters spiritual renewal. It is only with an experiential understanding of Nature that we can genuinely offer the reverence she merits and, as a result, feel our soul evolve in her silent embrace.

My psychotherapy practice has been most effective when I have journeyed to the remote regions of Montana, Wyoming, and Guatemala to support patients in their healing process. Without the availability of cell phone or internet service, and with no television or radio stations to distract us, the focus moves inward. After a predictable period of technological withdrawal, the imagined intrusions of gadgetry almost feel profane. In the sacred folds of the mountains, patients sensuously soak up Nature's healing balm. A wholeness and harmony develop—the essential spiritual starting point in any healing process. Patients begin to listen with inward ears and see with inward eyes, becoming aware with their whole beings, rather than being limited by the customary five (of many) senses.

Floating on Our Mother

Nature is an unlicensed psychotherapist, thank goodness! Her presence alone heals the agitated mind. This was the repeated observation of Minnesota naturalist and author Sigurd Olson. He wrote: "The outdoors has a way of healing and solving problems and works best where no conscious attempt is made, where no interpretation of any of its moods is even thought of at the time. Somehow, and sooner or later, we begin to discover that unconsciously during the time we were out, problems [were] being solved for us."[1]

Like the Ojibwa Indians who lived in the far north of North America, with its many forests and waterways, Olson fell in love with Minnesota's vast network of rivers and lakes, exploring them endlessly in his canoe. He wondered if the indigenous Ojibwa found similar peace floating on the heaving and subsiding belly of the Mother. He said of the canoe: "It is an antidote to insecurity. It provides a door to waterways of the past and a way of life with profound and abiding satisfactions. When a man is part of his canoe, he is part of all that canoes and men have ever known."[2]

Olson also reminded his readers that the preservation of wilderness must now be regarded as a humanitarian effort. His conclusion was based on the knowledge that humankind has lived in a natural environment for far more than 99 percent of its history, and that its physiological and psychic needs arise from this environment and are healed by it. A land ethic is, in fact, a human ethic.

That, too, is the wisdom of traditional healers. While humans dance to the music of the day, we still move, sway, heal, and are guided by ancient rhythms. We are still pregnant with Earth's teachings and are only in the early stages of our gestation period, albeit momentarily derailed by this thing called "progress." Yet, our prognosis remains hopeful as the resurgence in shamanic healing portends. Dr. Richard Gerber, a Michigan internist and student of indigenous healing, has said, "The discoveries we are making today are, in fact, reincarnational expressions of older spiritual knowledge which originated in ancient yet advanced civilizations."[3]

The shamanic way helps us to dismember, in order to remember and *re*-member. We may have to shed some of our technological toys each year, like a deer sheds its antlers, to start growing anew. Such is the way of Nature when we return to her for healing.

Grounded on
Mother Earth

Have you ever lived very close to someone and never known of their gifts until you moved away? Well, that was the case with Clint Ober and me. I resided in northern Wyoming, and he made his home in southern Montana. We were a short drive from each other, and both of us frequently visited the Crow Indian Reservation of Montana, which was between our two homes. Despite similar interests, our paths had never crossed. Both of us were so busy making money in our respective professions that work, not spirituality, consumed us. Neither of us felt spiritually anchored.

Then, one day in the summer of 2012, I sought out Clint after reading his extraordinarily enlightening book, *Earthing*. The title refers to a direct human connection with Mother Earth. This connection allows her electrical energy to reset our bodily frequencies in harmony with our planetary home and, from that electrical rootedness, we experience wellness. Clint likens this feminine energy to the coherence and cadence over which the conductor of a large orchestra presides.

I asked if I might interview Clint for an article that I wanted to present to *Sacred Hoop* magazine, a magazine on shamanism and indigenous healing based in the United Kingdom. He eagerly obliged. That is when some magic occurred; we poured out our hearts to each other, and tears were shed; tears that came from a deep resonance after sharing our most meaningful spirituality with each other and feeling the mutual respect that came with it. The bridge was Mother Earth, the catalyst was Native American cosmology, and the power came from heartfelt personal disclosures. The result, minus most of the warm sentiments, was revealed in the following adaptation of the *Sacred Hoop* 2013 article. It is the story of a businessman who, like many shamanic healers, fell apart before coming together in a new and strengthened way, with many gifts to be shared. I was reminded of my journey to Africa, where I discovered a more authentic version of myself, shed the career I had known with its predictability and financial security, and returned to reassemble myself into a more reverent healer.

Clint Ober is a modest man who wouldn't want any of his personal qualities embellished. Yet upon interviewing him, I was aware of how many elements of Joseph Campbell's hero's journey are revealed in Clint's life story. A classic hero's journey has, at minimum, four key stages:

Stage one commences with a *call to adventure*, when an individual feels a strong premonition and calling, a compelling desire to commit to a persona quest, an adventure into the unknown and unfamiliar when death is faced, figuratively or even literally. The hero senses everything familiar is about to change, but often the call is initially resisted or postponed. Ultimately an initiation unfolds when the near-death of body, ego, or an agonizing lifestyle must be faced squarely.

At stage two, the individual takes a *leap of faith*; he departs on the adventure, entering the natural world where trials and sacrifices are encountered.

As stage three unfolds, often the journey entails meeting *helpers*, especially female forms—like goddesses—that convey important messages. Symbols are revealed, challenging forces are engaged, and a more divine, unified, and spirit-filled way of life takes shape. New freedoms are experienced by engaging in a more reverent, service-driven lifestyle.

At the end of the journey, the fourth stage, the hero achieves the *return* to the everyday world, integrating and sharing his accumulated wisdom with others. Now he is capable of mastering clashing worlds—the old and the new, the profane and the sacred.[1]

The Enterpreneur

With the publication of his seminal book, *Earthing*, Clint Ober burst onto the healing scene in 2010. Beneath the sage healing advice in his book, there is also an underlying transformative story—modern mythology, if you will—of how Nature speaks to us and through us. How Nature, more than any physician or drug, can heal us.

From his seventeen years of entrepreneurial experience in the cable-television industry, Clint learned that a vibrant television picture, one without interference, depends upon the entire cable system being grounded in the earth. If the natural world can help humanity's electrical inventions operate better, he surmised, it could likely help the human mind and body restore itself to optimal functioning. Unfortunately, Clint observed, humans tend to insulate themselves from direct contact with the Source, Mother Earth. Our species, especially in the twenty-first century, prefers to stay indoors, and we wear "protective," rubber-soled shoes. Our Western lifestyle effectively separates us from Earth's invisible balancing and sustaining energy, which creates a super-abundance of inflammatory physical illnesses, while agitating our brains and emotions.

As a very successful businessman, Clint experienced the "good life," accumulating and consuming massive amounts of stuff. With this propensity, he spent an inordinate amount of time managing all his possessions. Eventually Clint became a slave to them; his possessions ultimately owned him. Clearly being impacted by this lifestyle, Clint's physical health deteriorated, and in 1993 he almost died. An experimental surgery was successful and gave Clint some added years on the planet. He committed to use that time to reassess all parts of his life and chart a new path. Upon discharge from the hospital, Clint awakened one morning at home with the profound sense that Earth was communicating with him. His near-death experience conveyed a message to live in harmony with the natural rhythms of the world. Spirit's voice was sudden and revealing—an epiphany.

Instantly, Clint felt an aversion to owning anything. Simultaneously, he noted how colors appeared deeper and more vibrant, and he had the realization that everything, absolutely everything, was energy. Clint's newly opened heart—plus his scientific training and common sense—had positioned him to receive this primordial calling, to reconnect with the earth for personal healing, and ultimately to serve his fellow man in more meaningful ways. He immediately began formulating a new life trajectory, quickly shedding nearly all of his personal belongings. Most of his material goods were given to family members over the next ninety days. No longer did Clint feel encumbered by his possessions.

With a newfound sense of liberation, Clint set out on a quest for a life with greater purpose and more integrity in line with his values. Over the ensuing two years, he immersed himself in Nature, traveling to many of America's national parks. But full clarity of his vision and destiny would be delayed. What he was jettisoning was very clear, but what was yet to be absorbed and integrated was not yet in perfect focus.

Giving Birth to Earthing

Many of Clint's eventual insights, as he later expressed in his book, *Earthing*, originated from his close observation of and familiarity with Native American healing traditions. As a child, he grew up near the Crow and Northern Cheyenne Indian Reservations. He recalls visiting the homes of Native friends. Upon arriving at a young boy's home one day after school, a Crow mother poignantly advised Clint at the door: "Take off your shoes, they'll make you sick." Additionally, he remembers the sister of a classmate who was suffering from scarlet fever. To promote her healing, the child's grandfather dug an earthen pit, placed the girl in the hole, built a fire nearby, and prayerfully stayed at her side for several days while she rested and slept until she had fully recovered.

Reflecting on many Native influences during his formative years, Clint concluded, "They looked at the world entirely differently. They lived more in Spirit, with everything being their cousin—the trees, the animals, blades of grass. They taught me that you shouldn't harm things. You respect all life. Ownership of anything is a foreign concept to Native Americans."

Clint recalled camping in Montana as a young man, feeling as though he were reuniting with Earth, becoming more centered, calm, and at one with the Spirit of place. "When I'm in similar locations today," he elaborated, "I feel a presence—something cleansing, uplifting, and quieting to the soul and mind. It's that sacredness of being one with the trees, grass, and critters, capturing glimpses of what this world is really about. It's a balance that is missing from our lives. Nowadays, people are so disconnected from Spirit, by that I mean *Nature*." With those thoughts, our sense of shared spirit reached a crescendo, and we quietly cried together.

A lifelong art lover and one-time serious collector, Clint was deeply touched by images and themes of an acquaintance, the late Native American Crow artist, Earl Biss. He purchased several of his paintings, including one favorite entitled *Escaping through a Hole in the Sky* that portrays several warriors preparing to ride horses skyward, departing Mother Earth, adventuring into the unknown. The depiction always spurred Clint's desire to commune more deeply with Spirit. Its appeal was not surprising, as Clint had spent much of his adult life swept up in contemporary American culture where success is measured by an attachment to money and belongings, not by integrity and meaning. He was intensely unhappy on that path. Clint mused, "When you are not attuned with the Spirit of Nature, living in this world can be crazy and torturous." For years, Biss's images have symbolized a subtle and continuous "calling"—Clint saw in them an unopened window that could provide escape from some of life's anguish by reconnecting with something bigger.

For two years after his surgery, Clint continued to travel throughout the West, reflecting on new occupational opportunities and Native American teachings. He concluded, "Everything in our environment is electrical first, then chemical. You must have an electronically stable living environment so that body and mind can function as they were designed to do."

Living in a tipi was one way that Native people stayed grounded traditionally, much like the Bushmen of Africa. Generally speaking, only in the last few hundred years have we humans moved into wooden, steel, and concrete dwellings and begun wearing rubber and plastic-soled footwear.

The result, Clint says, is that "we have disconnected from our ever-present ground state, our source of stability. Everything in the body—our organs, cells, and even thoughts—is energy, and because it is energy, it is electrical.

"While we all are trained and entrained by contemporary culture," he went on, "we have gone too far in one extreme, disconnecting from Earth. This world is crazy, and we all need a space for healing. Earth provides an energy field, a Spirit. When connected to her, your body conducts that energy and resonates with it. And it also emanates from you. Then you and Earth become one; you are the same. You are as big as Earth electrically, spiritually, and energetically. When you reconnect with Nature and open up, you shift and exit a window to a different place. The concept of *earthing* is about this truth. The point is to take our shoes off and touch Earth, to put our hands on Earth and attune to Her. I want people to look at Her and realize that Earth is not simply dirt; we are part of the Whole—Earth—up and walking around. Awakening others to this reality is now my mission."

Ancient African Energy Healing

Clint and I discussed some ancient Bushmen healing methods: Weekly, some of the remaining traditional San and !Kung Bushmen circle up and, while barefoot on the sand, draw from the earth's electrical field to heal one another. In their Giraffe Dance, Bushmen physically link up with one another as energy units, hands on each other's shoulders, oscillating, passing restorative num energy forward. Ultimately, the energy arrives at an ill person, who is suddenly jolted by the electrical force, often thrown to the ground unconscious, and soon thereafter transformed and healed—as if a reset button was pressed. In Hinduism, this life force is known as *kundalini* energy and as *prana*, and it has many other names varying from culture to culture.

Clint said, "I totally, totally understand what the Bushmen are doing when they touch each other in healing ceremonies! Because we aren't grounded as the ancient ones were, we are influenced primarily by unnatural forces. The body becomes more perturbed. Earth provides an electrical envelope to ground and stabilize us. It acts as an umbrella, shielding us from the intra-electrical instability of the body so that it can return to normal."

Expounding on cultures that don't regularly plant themselves firmly on Earth, Clint said, "When you are not grounded, your shield is down, leaving you more susceptible to stresses that disrupt normal, easy, natural body functioning. The mind becomes irritated. A loop is created that sends signals back to the body, which releases chemicals such as cortisol. Then the body gets out of whack; chaos prevails, allowing the manifestation of diseases and disorders. So, when you ground the body it is very much an automatic self-healing machine, operating 24/7 to maintain homeostasis and protect itself from pathogens." That helps to explain the surprisingly good health of the Hadza Bushmen, who walk barefoot and sleep on the ground. Even their structures are made only of thatch, which does not insulate them from Earth's electrical healing field.

"Grounding restores you to normal, quiets the mind and body, strengthens the immune system, and protects the body," Clint went on. "This remembered wellness is embedded in every cell. Grounding reduces the static, the noise, and the stress, allowing internal healing to take place."

Women and Grounding

"In recent years," Clint reflected, "I've noticed that when I ground women, they intuitively know what is happening. I don't have to explain anything. They know there is a connection between themselves and Earth. As soon as they place their feet on Earth, there is the recognition that they are a part of it. They experience it and become different very, very quickly. And they open up.

"Men, on the other hand, are warriors, always on guard, chasing whatever it is we are chasing. It seems absurd to most men that if you take your shoes off and plant your feet on Earth, it will provide any health benefits. Men are reluctant to put their bare feet on the ground, thinking, 'No way! I'll get my feet dirty.' If I ask a woman to do the same thing, I'm usually met with a smile."

Spirit regularly speaks to Clint, often in female form. He explained, "For years, when I lie down at night and am about to fall asleep, I slip into a meditative state. At those times I understand the earthing connection best. Images or visions come into my mind. I see eyes looking at me. Many of them are women [the goddess calling]. The demeanor on their faces, especially in their eyes, is that of pain. And they seem to be waiting for me. This has created a feeling of urgency in me to serve. Alone at night with my thoughts, I am connected to something much bigger than myself, something greater than any cultural influence."

Independent research is documenting an ever-increasing number of health benefits from earthing. Clint notes that many people in America are focused on "a pill for every ill, formulas and potions, while earthing teaches people that health is natural, our most natural state. Wellness is a byproduct of staying connected to Mother."

American Culture and Earthing

The connection with Earth, and the health benefits she conveys, begin immediately and are often felt within a few minutes. Clint said, "This whole thing we talked about in the book, *Earthing,* is more of a spiritual thing, Earth talking through me. In Nature, I am able to get into Spirit. Now, everything is more alive and more vibrant—the trees and everything. I find myself avoiding cities as much as possible. Today when I enter a house, I feel as if I'm going into a prison; it feels like some place I have to go to and take care of.

"Our culture has an American dream in which everyone shops. For example, after 9/11 the government urgently pleaded for Americans to go to the malls and shop. That urging rang loudly about our culture. The more we reduce consumption and accumulation, the more time we have to spend in Spirit—in Nature. As we use up the planet's resources, we lose the energy and aliveness of people too. Finding a balance is important. The less we consume, the less we own, the more we are able to be happy, because we have removed the burden that comes with ownership. Less becomes more."

Return and Integration

Reflecting on his evolving worldview after having returned from what I refer to as his hero's journey, Clint had more to say. "Today, I look at life differently. I still have an aversion to owning things. I don't want to own anything. I've let go of the craziness in my world and opened up to Nature and Spirit. In this way, I believe I've been influenced by the Native Americans. In my 'heart of hearts' there is nobody I'm closer to than Native Americans. They understand what I am doing. I no longer want to make my life about owning things or making money. I don't want to go to my grave with a tombstone that reads: 'He was a great consumer.' I want to depart knowing that I have done something worthwhile, something good—that I wasn't just a taker."

We reflected on the trajectory of our lives and our career changes. I wanted to know more about his course now that he is marketing earthing devices and his new/ancient ideas are spreading like wildfire. With the back-to-Earth movement and a rekindling of ancient lifestyles, business is growing, an occurrence about which Clint has mixed feelings, given his financial "success" in his earlier life.

He clarified his thoughts by saying, "Today, I am challenged by the earthing movement because it has turned into a business. I recognize that it has to be this way; people need help grounding themselves. I simply allowed this to manifest. I just became open and available for Spirit to bring it about. Earthing is not about our products; it is really about connecting with Spirit. Nor is this whole movement about me. I'm not a guru. I'm not important. What *is* important is the natural world. Earthing is a message from Earth: 'Put your feet on me and it will help you stop, examine your existence, and ask yourself how it is that you live, where you live, and how you interact with others.' Best of all, the basic practice of earthing is free."

Heroism in the Second Half of Life

The great mythologist, Joseph Campbell, outlined the patterns found in stories of heroic journeys from culture to culture. Most have the same plot and the same meaning. They are not physical journeys of legendary persons but internal adventures. They are not about the discoveries of Ferdinand Magellan, Amelia Earhart, or Neil Armstrong but the rediscovery of parts of one's self and forgotten principles of the cosmos, perhaps as in the story of Saint Francis of Assisi. The catalyst behind a journey of discovery (or rediscovery) may be a restlessness or a life crisis, much like Clint experienced as death knocked on his door. Importantly, what makes the journey heroic is not just the risks that a person confronts but also the fact that he does it on behalf of everyone, not just himself. What is discovered, perhaps anew, is a strange, internal reality that has been avoided or overlooked for far too long. On a symbolic level, the individual develops deeper parts of himself while, at the same time, developing a greater sense of unity with the world around him, which is the ultimate nature of humanity in the largest sense. He discovers who he is beyond ego, self-promotion, accomplishments, or the accumulation of wealth.

One of the hero's goals, especially in the second half of life, is not separating from his roots—his homeland, his consciousness, his family—but reconnecting with unconscious archetypal forces that can no longer remain nascent. It is about solving personal and societal problems, about providing knowledge that relieves suffering and truly serves people. For those of us trained in psychology, the goal of the first half of life is the establishment of a strong and individuated ego. With a strong ego we can become independent and better accomplish personal goals. The goal of the second half of life, however, is not weakening the ego but rather using the ego's strength to set forth on a quest to refocus it and rejoin what Jung called the *collective unconscious*. The end result is usually an increased sense of harmony, a moral compass of enhanced clarity, and a growing desire to serve others—or, better said, serve the common humanity of which the person is now more deeply linked. The authentic hero discovers who he really is: Nature in a wrapping of skin. At the life juncture, fewer things are alien, fewer things can threaten him.

Like Clint, the hero is more modest after his tests. Even though he has been tested and survived, he is humbler as a result of recognizing his common humanity. He has come home and found that home to be bigger than ever imagined before. The choices to be made are of greater significance now than ever before. Purpose and meaning are alive in his soul. And his art collection and checkbook balance, trivial.

Journey to the Land of Souls

Traveling the world and learning from indigenous mentors, one can experience a romanticized temptation to shed the sport coats and the SUV and flee to the jungle in pursuit of a new and more meaningful life. It has been my personal conclusion, though, that I can offer the most to my profession and to my soul if I don't abandon ship but, instead, build bridges between the old and the new. For me, that entails preserving the best of both worlds, the current insights of psychological theories—a profession with only a hundred years of history—and the ancient truths of shamanic healers. Perhaps this way, today's Western knowledge can be expanded on a foundation of tried and tested methods, blending shamanic *best practices* with psychology's *best practice*. And when mystery and a reverent spirit are added to conventional techniques, healing possibilities can be unlimited. In fact, our patients may transcend previously unimagined boundaries.

What that can look like may be understood in Danny's story. A young teen from an Indian Reserve in Manitoba, Canada, Danny's development was limited presumably by fetal alcohol effects, PTSD, and a host of other psychologically ascribed labels. I learned that by allowing his intuition to direct his treatment of early-life traumas and challenge earthly realities, Danny could orchestrate his own healing. In this story you will see how, with the aid of a modern brain stimulator, he journeyed to another place and returned with insights and a calm that might otherwise have taken months of psychotherapy to cultivate. It is an account of how a guardian animal, Eagle, lifted Danny up and fostered a new perspective on his life.

Traditional Ojibwa Healing

Repeatedly, my shamanic peregrinations have taken me to the lakes and forests of Manitoba. I am blessed to be accepted into the Ojibwa community of Hollow Water, where my perspective on healing is always widened, deepened, and strengthened by their sacred orientation to Earth. In Hollow Water, the Ojibwa have consciously chosen to return to ancient healing approaches that augment, and sometimes even replace, contemporary Western healing practices that have sometimes been foisted upon them by governmental forces. Many times, I have written—in books and magazines—about how the community of Hollow Water uses traditional spiritual methods in dealing with cases of sexual abuse and other interpersonal abuses. Their focus is not so much on broken laws but on broken relationships. Restoring connections to others, to the tenets of the past, and to Nature can make a person whole again. Native beliefs require medicine people to demonstrate their efficacy, time and time again, before they are chosen to serve as the guide for someone in need of healing. And to become powerful community healers, they must use rituals embedded in sacred connections to the physical and animal world surrounding them, of which they believe they are an integral part and which Native peoples throughout North America describe as "all my relatives."

On a cold and snowy winter day in 2012, I once again found myself in the Community Holistic Circle Healing (CHCH) offices located in the tiny village of Hollow Water. In this setting, I have nurtured ties with my extended family, among them a fourteen-year-old boy, Danny, who has known severe internal turmoil for most of his short life. Danny's mother was addicted to alcohol and, while he was developing in her womb, Danny was already awash in liquor. Both his parents experienced tragic deaths when he was a young boy, leaving him abandoned. At least Danny had a sister with whom he remained attached. But then, a short time later, his sister suddenly died too.

A married couple, both healers at CHCH, adopted Danny, knowing full well the responsibilities before them would be challenging. Danny appeared to suffer not only from the grief of losing his entire family but also from the aforementioned fetal alcohol effects. Additionally, he seemed to have what some counselors would call attention deficit hyperactivity disorder (ADHD) but could also be seen as hypervigilance resulting from trauma. Because Danny was very impulsive and limited by developmental and learning disabilities, when I arrived I wasn't surprised to learn that he had recently dropped out of school and had started smoking for the calming effect that tobacco provided him. Like his natural parents, he was drawn by the allure of alcohol too.

Microcurrent Brain Stimulation

On prior visits to Hollow Water, I had packed my Alpha-stim machine, a microcurrent brain-stimulation device that calms the deep brain region (the limbic system) where fear, anxiety, and mood disorders arise. The machine has a remarkable ability to calm the amygdala, the basal ganglia, and, in general, the entire deep limbic system of the brain using alpha-wave activity. It has proven itself an effective (and FDA approved) way to quiet anxiety, reduce depression, treat insomnia, and arrest addictive urges. On prior visits, Danny had shown a curiosity about this device, asking many questions, and once asked me to affix the connecting clamps to his ears. His adoptive parents were confident that he would not be able to sit still for a full twenty-minute treatment, but because of his apparent motivation we forged ahead. Throughout the treatment he never moved. The sudden, powerful, and calming effect it produced was very pleasant for Danny. On my future visits to the community, he would ask if I had brought the machine with me, suggesting that he might want to experiment with it again. And we did.

When I returned in 2012, I had been away from the community for about a year. No one was told of my impending trip, but the night before my arrival Danny approached his parents and asked, "When is that guy with the white machine coming back?"

Danny's parents were surprised by his inquiry, and everyone except Danny was surprised to see my pickup pull into CHCH. Danny skipped school that morning to come looking for me. He had an uncanny ability to perceive things that were about to happen—perhaps on a unique frequency—picking up on communications that others without his talents routinely missed.

Upon arriving at the CHCH offices, he looked inside my vehicle, searching for the white machine. He noticed it, and, after a few hours of socializing, asked if we could use the machine to help him "focus and concentrate." I agreed to support his goal, and we retired to a quiet room in the building, far from the distracting sounds of other people. What unfolded was a privilege and an honor to observe. The experience further anchored me in the value of blending old and new ways of healing, using traditional spiritual-belief systems and contemporary clinical technologies.

In traditional Ojibwa culture, as with many aboriginal tribes of North America and other societies around the world, journeying into spirit lands is still a common practice; it is very different and more time consuming than the techniques taught to Western students of neoshamanism. This is especially true at Hollow Water, where they often spend days at a time on solo vision quests and fasts, during which they are quieted and centered by Mother Earth. During these ceremonies, a spirit helper or guardian animal spirit may appear to the person who is journeying, and the animal guide may help the journeyer navigate different realms as the person attempts to heal personal problems—emotional, physical, and, most of all, spiritual.

As external distractions are tuned out or shut off, a person is better able to commence an inward journey. Healing is most likely to occur in a state of altered consciousness, or what the Czech psychiatrist Stanislav Grof has termed a *holotropic state*, in which breathing patterns have been changed to encourage entry into other dimensions. When a person's eyes are closed, perceptual changes can occur; individuals can be flooded with imagery accompanied by emotions of rapture, bliss, transcendence, peace, calm, and unity. The themes of these visions are often drawn from an individual's personal history as well as his or her cultural worldview and teachings. But they may also derive from other sources: the cosmos, mythology, and the *over-self*—what some call the Greater Consciousness, the ultimate source of consciousness downloaded into the human brain and localized mind. These sources may be the basic stock of the part of the psyche that depth psychologist C. G. Jung referred to as the *collective unconscious,* previously unrealized understandings that arise from ancient shared memories unconsciously passed down from ancestors or from other unknown origins.

When Ojibwas enter an altered state—especially while they are directly in touch with Mother Earth—it readies them for an important event that is about to commence. Anticipation is felt and expectations rise. Within a thoughtfully choreographed setting, and with the appearance of a guardian sprit animal, the individual is ready to be an active cocreator of his journey into the Land of the Souls. It is in this realm that the ancient and deceased may be encountered, and, while in trance, that one's attention can be focused, often with a dialogue ensuing with one's inner sage or healer or with one's protective animal spirit. Because the Ojibwa are grounded in a life situated close to land that is still "undeveloped" by Western society, these spirits are more readily accessible, and healing sometimes comes rapidly when medicine people and their patients share a deep connection with Mother Earth. This is unlike almost any experience that unfolds over a weekend shamanic workshop.

In order for the altered state to be achieved, ideally there should be a genuine sense of being anchored in a sacred place that can carry and transport the supplicant. This idea may sound fanciful to some who are unfamiliar with these ways; because of their unfamiliarity and doubt, they may never discover the *sacred magic* of a journey. Danny, however, *was* familiar with the possibilities of being transported to other worlds; it had been repeated many times by the teaching of local elders and the conversations of his adoptive parents.

An earth-based healer can facilitate the activation of hibernating forces residing in Nature, in an individual, and in the spirit world. The patient often possesses deep but somewhat atrophied inner resources that need to be awakened by some sort of energy shift, whether that be through rituals, plant medicines, or a brain-stimulation device. Together, the medicine person or shaman, along with the animal spirits, provide a protective container, an exoskeleton of support that enables the patient to explore what might be regarded as dangerous or frightening emotional places. In doing so, fears and anxieties can be approached and released, often amid convulsive gyrations. Ultimately, a rebirth takes place, and a humble but confident sense of power develops, often revealing itself in the physical form of an animal spirit— perhaps with the confident gait of Grizzly Bear or the lightness of Hummingbird.

From his personal experiences, Danny knew he couldn't accomplish much in school, or in life, without improving his ability to concentrate. Much of his past formed a continuous background of distraction felt in the present. Additionally, he knew that a healing experience would not occur without quieting much of the mental chatter constantly racing through his mind. By inquiring of me, "Will ya wire me up?" Danny was saying, "I want to be able to focus and concentrate much better." And that focused attention could also enable him to reach an altered state, experience increased peace and harmony, and perhaps travel to whatever emotional landscape he needed to face. With his interest at heart, I asked Danny to close his eyes and practice some deep breathing with me, following the sounds of my breath, the audible exhales being longer than the inhales.

Departure to the Land of The Spirits

I placed the alpha-stim's clamps on Danny's earlobes, sending a very small 0.5Hz bipolar electrical current from one side of his brain to the other. The aim was to quiet and synchronize both sides of his brain. In less than two minutes, Danny was, by his account, "soaring," feeling as though he were floating off into space. He fell into a deep trance state in which very little was said. At one point, I noticed his eyes were fluttering rapidly and his arms and hands were quivering slightly, as if a vibratory energy was arising and moving though him—something he would not recollect later.

As his time on the machine continued, Danny seemed to pass through a scary segment. I softly interrupted with an inquiry, "What are you feeling?"

He responded with one word: "Fear."

I reassured him that he was in a safe place with a trusted friend and that such fears always pass. "Be brave," I suggested, and his internal focus resumed.

Deeper and deeper he retreated into himself. He was withdrawing from the everyday realm. Soon I noticed that Danny seemed very much at peace, approaching the suggestible hypnogogic state between the brain's alpha and theta brain-wave activity. It was at that point that his arms slowly rose from his side, opening wide as if he was soaring. Then his fingers curled rigidly, much like bird talons that were gripping onto something.

In a whisper, Danny announced, "I am riding on Eagle. There is a gate and graves." After a moment he added, "We are going in."

Anxiety became apparent, but not the fear of before. He became giddy, and then his emotions transformed into calm once again. With contentment evident on his face, I watched and waited in silence, curious about what exactly was happening and hopeful of a good outcome.

Returning with Insights to Be Shared

After approximately thirty minutes, with Danny's eyes remaining closed and the machine still operating, I asked him to imagine a blackboard in front of him and a piece of sky-blue chalk in his hand. I instructed him to write the word *calm* slowly on the board and stare at it for a short time to absorb the message while in his suggestible state. Then I encouraged him to open his eyes and return to the reality before him at CHCH. As Danny did open his eyes and collected his thoughts, I could tell that he was reoriented to the moment.

We sat quietly for a short time and then went upstairs, where his adoptive mother was sitting with two medicine people from the community. At first Danny stood silently staring out a window, looking toward the sky. He commented that his eyesight was incredibly sharp, like that of Eagle. Then, with a very quiet and peaceful demeanor, he sat down with us.

Everyone noted that Danny's face had a demonstrably different appearance. He wore a gentle smile. One person, who had known Danny all his life, silently mouthed the following words to me: "Who is that?" She was seeing a new person before her.

With measured words, Danny explained how Eagle had appeared to him in trance and had invited him to get on his back and depart for an important, but unknown, destination. Together, they flew over forest, rivers, and lakes, with Danny holding on tightly, in the gripping that I had noticed moments before. Danny recalled approaching a gate—in fact, the gate of the cemetery where his biological family is buried. He was far north of Hollow Water, near the community of Pauingassi where he once had lived.

Guided and protected by Eagle, they flew into what, indeed, looked like a cemetery. They had entered the Spirit World where the dead are not dead. There, Danny was greeted by his deceased father and mother. He had seen them approaching with smiles of delight, and they shared loving embraces. His parents shared reassuring words of their undying love for him, something that would never end. Even during tragic times and periods of turmoil, they said, he remained part of their world; they were always connected, and Danny had never been forgotten. During his journey, Danny clearly savored how much his parents still adored him and how much they missed him. He was important, after all.

Continuing to recount his travel, Danny explained how, even amid the journey, he was aware that his parents were living in another dimension and that he would eventually have to return to his far different, everyday, middle-world existence at Hollow Water. Then he explained to his further delight how his deceased sister appeared. Another heartwarming reunion occurred. He was now connected to his entire family, both over time and location, as if neither dimension existed to hamper his travel. With the power born of Eagle, Danny concluded that he could always revisit the Spirit World as needed to be reassured that he wasn't alone or forgotten. And with those final comforting images, he chose to depart Spirit World on the wings of Eagle. He was ready to resume his other life.

Danny recalled flying part of the way back to Hollow Water on Eagle, not feeling the need to grip so tightly. With growing confidence, he became one with Eagle and began soaring on his own. He delicately managed the thermals, always being careful not to overcorrect. He looked down and saw familiar locations: Grand Rapids, Bloodvein, and Pine Falls. Gently, he descended to the ground with the skill he learned from Eagle. Awaiting him on the shoreline were his adoptive mother and father, along with a tribal healer. He greeted them all with hugs. Danny also reflected on the love he enjoyed from his adoptive parents. In essence, Danny concluded upon his return that he had the best of both worlds—love on each side.

Eagle is a frequent visitor in Ojibwa society and is frequently seen soaring over ceremonies and sacred places around Hollow Water First Nation. He helps with the rebirthing process and is a symbol of strength, courage, and protection. His vision is sharp; Eagle always sees the bigger picture from his elevated position. As Jung insightfully wrote, "Nature, the world of instincts, takes the child on its wings [where] it is nourished and protected by animals."

Months later

For years, Danny had been encouraged to take symptom-suppressing medications prescribed by white physicians and psychologists. He had been placed in a special classroom, without his exceptional hidden skills of healing being recognized. Conventional treatment approaches were of little help. Since his journey, the verdict is still being awaited. Those who have known Danny the longest say that he now acts and speaks in a much calmer fashion. "He's happier," they say.

Although Hollow Water is steeped in sacred traditions, the community remains open to complimentary modern technologies as well as healing practices from cultures all over the world. Their medicine tradition, the *Medewiwin*, is a powerful medicine of the imagination blended with the knowledge of the animals and plant relatives. The old natural ways provide safe passage to the inner landscapes of the mind.

We all have the makeup—the latent natural instincts—that were long ago developed to promote self-healing, whether we are recovering from a simple skin abrasion or a devastating sense of soul loss following sexual abuse. (It might be more accurate to say soul *wounding*, for it is questionable that anyone actually loses one's soul; but *soul loss* is the term widely used by shamanic healers.) Our animal relatives haven't been as quick to forget these self-healing abilities as we have in the Western world, nor have many indigenous cultures. A worldwide revitalization is now occurring. Nature has fashioned humans in a way that, when we are in proper harmony with all our relatives, we can remember wellness and return to that healthy state. Danny's sudden insights and potential transformation are proof. His experience is similar to that of a traditional shamanic initiation—from being broken to being reassembled by an inner healing wisdom. It may one day culminate with Danny being recognized as the wise healer of others. Already young people in Hollow Water are talking about him. What others may see as disabilities they see as special abilities. I wonder: will he be a medicine man one day?

Western Demystification

Upon hearing of Danny's satisfying journey, a psychologist approached me, asking, "Do you know what *really* happened?" While he was not from the reserve and had never met Danny, he was eager to apply familiar theories that would make sense of the experience, at least for him. He explained that Western psychology could explain the "so-called journey" according to the principles of terror management theory (TMT).[1]

TMT is used to explain how our psychological defense mechanisms address the terror arising from our realization that death is, after all, inevitable and irrevocable, despite our instinct for self-preservation. Many people in the face of death (their own or others) have the need for reassurance that they will one day be reunited with lost loved ones. They hope to diminish or get past their grief with a sense of well-being in the certainty that their connection with departed loved ones will endure. In Danny's case, the warm and welcoming reunion he had with his parents bolstered his sense of living up to parental ideals of being a good son. Such a reunion can restore a sense of worthiness and assuage feelings of abandonment.

TMT asserts that, for people to manage the terror of death effectively, they must rely on cultural beliefs and values (such as a Spirit World), as well as on time-tested practices, to treat themselves while in a personally engineered altered state or following a near-death experience. When bad things happen, people want to imbue their world with meaning and may even confabulate a narrative that provides a more coherent and satisfying worldview.

So, the Ojibwa explanation would be that Danny did, indeed, journey to the Spirit World and see his parents, facilitated by

Eagle, while the view of Western psychology would be that the experience was all a defense mechanism to protect him from the terror of loss in death. But whatever explanation is offered—that of traditional Ojibwa spirituality or of Western psychology—what can't become lost in theory is the fact that Danny healed himself. At some conscious level, he knew there was an internal physician residing in him. His time-tested and culturally supported belief system was his own "good medicine." I simply accompanied Danny on the journey of his own making. That is the beauty of indigenous healing; mystery doesn't have to be reduced to theoretical explanations from other cultures.

Peruvian Plant-Medicine Shamanism

It is common for friends and colleagues to approach me with a rather generic request: "Gerry, if you ever need someone to carry your luggage on a trip, I'm available." Truth is, I much prefer to travel alone, unencumbered by anyone else's agenda. I am accustomed to staying in one spot for days, if I find a fascinating culture, a powerful shaman, or beautiful scenery. There have been a few times when I have given in to the requests of others, introducing them to rich cultural experiences and healing experiences. Friends from Sweden, Nicaragua, Canada, Washington, DC, and Montana have been such exceptions. Their interests seemed sincere: they wanted more than a getaway; they sought a cultural immersion.

Then there was the case of Chris from Iowa. Chris and I have both worked extensively in the trauma field and were curious if jungle plant medicines truly were effective. Chris, however, had a more personal interest. He was in his fifties and suffered from a significant hearing loss. He wondered if ayahuasca might restore some of his hearing. Of course, I could make no promises, but I did explain how shamans tend to believe that there is no disease that arises on Pachamama (Mother Earth) for which there is no remedy. I told Chris that the *curanderos* say, "Nothing is impossible if you believe." With that slight reassurance, Chris was "all in," and we booked our flights to Iquitos, Peru, a large, yet surprisingly remote city available only by plane or river-boat travel.

Chris explained to me that his lifestyle was not particularly edgy, yet he was open to being stretched. He was fascinated by tales from the Peruvian jungle of shamans who used exotic plant medicines (entheogens) such as ayahuasca (*Banisteriopsis caapi*)—also

FIGURE 7. Q'ero Shaman, Peruvian Andes. The Q'ero live close to the sky, the source of cosmic wisdom. (Author's photograph)

referred to as *yagé*, or, casually, *aya*—and the cactus San Pedro (*Echinopsis peruviana*) to expand consciousness and heal all sorts of ailments, physical and emotional, including trauma. Having been to the High Andes Mountains before with medical anthropologist Alberto Villoldo on a trip I would define as spiritual tourism, I, myself, had experienced only a cursory introduction to the rituals and healing practices of the Q'ero tribe in the Peruvian Andes, but I had not yet been exposed to any tribes in the Amazon basin.

It was time for something more intimate, adventurous, and culturally true. I sought guidance from Carlos Tanner, founder of the Ayahuasca Foundation in Iquitos. His connections to legitimate Shipibo shamans (curanderos familiar with folk medicine) were impressive. He knew the authentic ones.

Carlos actually hails from the United States; he adopted a more Latin-sounding name after studying for several years in Peru under a well-known and respected shaman, Don Juan, who lived in Iquitos. He felt more at home in the jungle than in the northeastern United States with all its hubbub.

Arrival at the Iquitos Camp

After Chris and I landed in Iquitos, a small van transported us out of town and to the edge of the jungle. From there we hiked in a short distance to what would be our home for the next ten days. Carlos warmly greeted us at the camp and showed us to our sleeping quarters, a screened room next to several outhouses. Depending on the breeze and the time of day, the sounds and smells could be special.

Then there were the beds. All we could find, at first, were frames with springs. *Did they forget we were coming?* we wondered. Eventually we scored a couple of mattresses with years of stains and permeated with the humid smells of the jungle. A thin sheet was placed atop each one to give the appearance of a sanitary barrier. A second sheet would keep some of the insects, especially the giant moths, from landing directly on us. Sleeping was, at least for me, a wonderful experience as the jungle sounds of insects and birds wafted through the atmosphere. Chris was not so happy, asking if there were an air-conditioned hotel back in Iquitos to which we might return each night. I chose not to reply and hoped his discomfort would pass. It didn't help, however, to be awakened one morning to loud screams from the neighboring room. A young woman from Spain—a solo traveler—was sleeping alone when a tarantula crossed her bed. Little comfort was provided by the two local women who came running to her aid, only to flee screaming upon sight of the giant spider.

Vine of the Soul

The outdoor "kitchen," where all the food was prepared, was predominantly a large, wooden table occasionally wiped clean with soap and water. Rodents darted in and out of the area, apparently preferring our diet to their own.

Carlos had prescribed a special *dieta* for us of vegetables and greens seasoned with little more than lemon juice. A few local fruits, low in sugar, complemented the meals. It was also important to avoid certain foods such as salt, sugar, and meat. And alcohol was forbidden, as was sex.

The goal of the special diet is to ready the body with the spirits of the plant world, eventually introducing the ayahuasca vine and *chacruna* leaves (*Psychotria viridis*). *Ayahuasca* is often referred to as the "vine of the dead," perhaps better understood as the "vine of the souls," but people familiar with the plant prefer to think of it as a medicinal ally. It comes alive when blended with the psychoactive ingredient dimethyltryptamine, usually referred to as DMT, contained in chacruna and in *chagraponga*—another Amazonian plant. Tobacco (*mapacho*) smoke can also be a part of the mixture. Typically, it is blown into the crown of the head and over the face. It is said to clear the energy field, form a layer of protection, potentiate aya, and maintain visions. Plants are regarded as part of Pachamama's skin, each having its own spirit and a consciousness of its own that can infuse us with the wisdom arising from Nature.

Americans have long been afraid of aya because it creates a variety of altered states. It is sometimes referred as a psychedelic, but aya may be better understood as a *psychointegrator*. Such medicines work, in part, by boosting serotonin to manifest psychological healing of emotionally painful experiences. The result is a greater sense of connectedness with all life forms, allowing people to integrate traumatic experiences successfully.

In short, ayahuasca uncovers and works with what is in you. By that I mean it introduces you to hidden realities within yourself, to your own internally created visions rather than to some totally unnatural, foreign vision. I often liken it to the fourth step in Alcoholics Anonymous, because aya can force you painfully to relive and purge some of your most despicable deeds with terrifying visions before delivering you to the other side and peace. Aya can be seen as a plant agent that changes your vibratory nature—your persistent but not very healthy energy state. It has long been illegal in the United States due to politically inspired scare tactics. Nevertheless, it is still sought after by recreational drug users, medical anthropologists, and serious spiritual seekers.

In contrast to how an SSRI antidepressant works, drinking the aya brew quickly and dramatically elevates serotonin levels. When serotonin rises to very high levels, there may be excessive stimulation of the vagus nerve. In the West, this phenomenon is sometimes diagnosed as serotonin syndrome. It is thought to be responsible for much of the vomiting (*la purga*) that ensues upon drinking the aya brew, as well as the eventual profound feelings of equanimity, and unity—a sense of merging with a greater force and with all that is. Conventional psychologists warn of this phenomenon, and *ayahuasqueros* (shamans who use ayahuasca for healing) encourage it.

Brazilian researchers have looked at the prevalence of mental health disorders while contrasting Amazonian indigenous cultures where *ayahuasca* is routinely imbibed (even by pregnant women and children) and where it is not used at all. The striking results revealed that where ayahuasca use is a formalized and ritualized part of a society, far fewer mental illnesses are seen. Ayahuasca-using subjects appeared more confident, outgoing, optimistic, relaxed, carefree, uninhibited, cheerful, energetic and, interestingly, stubborn. Long-term ayahuasca users demonstrate significantly higher scores on measures of concentration and short-term memory. Said another way, this entheogen may have a preventive effect.

The afflicted will pilgrimage to Iquitos with the hopes of being relieved of long-standing maladies, like Chris who wanted his hearing restored. Most of these persons report frustration with prior treatments in clinic and hospital settings. Still others who have been burdened with addictions and interpersonal trauma (especially sexual abuse) have not responded to conventional treatment regimens and have reported that several ayahuasca treatments are comparable to years of psychotherapy. The key is *set* and *setting*. When the treatment is provided in aya's home, and when sacred ceremony accompanies its administration, treatment outcomes are always better. In this way, aya can shift a person from being distrustful and adversarial to embracing life, often quite quickly.

Water-Spirit Energy

Having previously met with an African water-spirits healer, I was intrigued to know what common features existed between African and Amazonian shamans. Cornering Carlos one day, I blurted out what even to me sounded like an odd question: Given that energy shifts are essential to altering the health of a patient, could electric eels have a restorative role equal to that of plant medicines?

Carlos looked surprised at my inquiry. Quickly he responded, "Yes, but what leads you to ask that question? Nobody has ever asked me that before."

I didn't really know; it had been an intuitive thought on my part, bubbling up from somewhere.

That was the beginning of a marvelous discussion! Carlos explained that years ago his *maestro* (mentor), Don Juan, had encouraged Carlos to strengthen his healing powers by charging his body with the power of Eel. It entailed having the energy of an electric eel surgically implanted into his body. The first task was to capture an eel and keep it alive in a pail until it was time for the surgical procedure the following day. After the eel was captured, Carlos was instructed to grip it in his hand to absorb the sting of its voltage. Grimacing, he was unable to do so for more than a minute. Carlos dropped the eel on the dirt, only to pick it up bravely again and undergo the transmission of energy one more time. In that way, an intimate connection was made between the eel and Carlos. It was a bequeathing of the energy of Eel—a sharing of power—that would live on in Carlos's body until his passing.

It seems as though whichever culture I visit, a goal of all healers is to borrow strength from the animal world to improve their ability to serve patients. Working alone, they may grow fatigued from the exhausting responsibilities of caring for the ill. But, they explain, with the help of powerful animals—whether it be Whale, Jaguar, Grizzly Bear, Lion, etc.—their energy is raised to a higher level with the increased chance that it will be maintained longer. It is about merging with a greater source. And the eel had powerful energy that, when merged with Carlos's personal vibration, would portend a promising future for him as an ayahuasquero or a *vegetalista* (one who works with medicinal plants), both of which were goals that Carlos had set for himself.

I have since seen a video of the surgery itself. It is not for the fainthearted. First, an assistant lit some candles to signify the beginning of what was an important ceremony. The process began with the eel still alive, in order to capture as much of its energy as possible before implanting it in Carlos's left forearm. I watched Don Juan carefully dissect a stringy piece of the eel's spine and set it aside. The muscles of the eel were still relaxing while it was being filleted as its life began to depart. Don Juan was doing this on bare ground in his yard, while dogs played amid the men. While Carlos nervously awaited the implant, some token alcohol was smeared on his arm, but Don Juan didn't appear to use any. Obviously, these people have different values regarding sanitation.

Nothing was administered to mediate pain. With Carlos sitting in a lawn chair, Don Juan threaded the eel's spine with a needle and pushed the needle with the spine attached through Carlos's skin, near a major vein, until it broke through the skin on the other side of the arm several inches away. Snip, snip with a scissors to remove loose ends, and the procedure was complete. No complications or ensuing infection were reported. With bacteria to be found everywhere outdoors and especially around animals, curiously people in Peru seem more resistant to illness than in our highly antiseptic culture. Bodies adapt with proper bacterial flora in their intestines. That is the message of a contemporary Western physician, Josh Axe, in his paradigm-busting book, *Eat Dirt*.[1]

An Introduction to Wild-Plant Medicines

While in preparation for a series of ayahuasca ceremonies, I had ample time to explore the jungle. I walked through the rainforest with Don Lucho, a *mestizo* (mixed blood) ayahuasquero who has studied plants in numerous countries. He regards plants as embodiments of conscious, intelligent beings—his teachers. When they are ingested, their wisdom is incorporated, and it guides him in his work with patients.

On our walk, Don Lucho stopped for a moment and inquired about a slight limp evident in my gait. I explained that, after years of marathon running, I had a significant amount of discomfort in my knees; in the States, my physician had suggested surgery as the remedy. As we walked on together, I watched Don Lucho tear leaves from plants, sniffing and biting into them as if to identify them accurately. Large amounts ended up in a bag without any explanation as to what he was gathering. At other times, he would dig out a root and drop it into his bag.

Much later that day, Don Lucho returned to camp looking for me. From a large variety of leaves and roots he had pressed a small amount of liquid that was designed to be a liniment. Among the key constituents were wild garlic and wild capsaicin, the latter a chili pepper. He smeared the green liquid on my knees, and immediately I felt a penetrating heat. Still later, Don Juan returned to inquire if the medicine was helpful. Indeed it was, I assured him.

On another occasion, I was fortunate to assist in the preparation of aya for an opening ceremony. Don Lucho made his own brew from the vine near his home and, under supervision, another batch was prepared onsite. The day-long process entails cutting and pounding the vine into a fibrous pulp to help it release its chemicals. It was slowly boiled in water, with the thick, dark residue being drained off and saved. Second and third rounds of water were added to extract all of the plant's medicine. A chef would call this process a *reduction*. Later, the leaves of chacruna (or a similar plant) were added to activate the medicine. I was asked to pray over the brew for the entire morning and afternoon, my peaceful healing intentions becoming a part of the mixture. I took this responsibility seriously, as about ten of us were going to drink the brew inside the healing hut (*maloca*), and I wanted everyone to have a good experience that night.

The Ceremony

After days—and for many, weeks—of dietary preparation and abstinence from alcohol and sex, it was time for the first ceremony. There were to be several ceremonies altogether, and we would have the luxury of having a different shaman guide the proceedings each time, every shaman with his own special concoction. There are many kinds of aya, some bringing about a lightness of spirit and sense of elevation, while others can foster powerful purges and unpleasant imagery before bestowing their ultimate rewards.

In the dark of the jungle night, when even the moon's light couldn't penetrate the jungle canopy, all lights and candles were extinguished. The anticipation was quietly intense. We all put cushions on the floor to sit on, knowing we would be there for a least six hours. Just as the shaman had set his altar with only a single candle for light, a participant calmly asked for the lights to be turned on, as he felt something on his body. A tarantula was walking over his legs. One of the helpers grabbed a broom and gently swept the giant spider to the door, opened the door, and waited for the tarantula to step outside. During the brief moment of illumination, I decided to investigate the tickling sensation on my back. As I leaned forward, a huge moth flew away, perhaps three or four inches in length; it had the shape of a stealth bomber.

When the lights were dimmed again, one by one we approached the shaman, kneeled before him, and were poured some of the brew in a cup. All of us had been told in advance that the taste would be repugnant. Just gulp it down fast, we were advised, no sipping. The best way I can describe the taste is to compare it with a very strong Starbucks coffee that has sat on a burner for many hours until incredibly bitter, with a splash of battery acid and some sawdust added. Its thick, muddy consistency allowed its essence to linger interminably in the mouth. I was the first person asked to approach the altar; and, after Carlos and the shaman had a discussion in Spanish (during which I recall hearing the word *mucho*), a second dose was given to me. I never fully understood why, as the others all were given just one serving. Perhaps it had to do with the fact that I had been intimately involved in the brew's preparation.

Within twenty minutes, I'm sure people across the floor could hear the lion's roar from my stomach. Aya was doing its job of gathering up unhealthy guests and preparing them for expulsion. In the next ten or fifteen minutes, all that could be heard was nonstop vomiting and groaning. Everyone had their assigned pail between their legs and must have been anxious for this facet of the ceremony to conclude.

Then silence set in. Occasionally, someone would be compelled to speak, much as in a Quaker meeting. Throughout, the shaman shook ties of leaves, creating a steady whoosh, whoosh, whoosh backdrop. His *icaros* (songs) seemed endless. They were highly varied and personalized; the intention was to create and hold sacred space, while providing comfort and guiding our experience. In the night, the shaman approached everyone at least once. His ingestion of the brew gave him the ability to look into our bodies, as if having X-ray eyes. With the information gleaned, additional prayerful icaros were sent our way along with smoke, and then more smoke from his big mapacho cigarettes. Never had I had so much smoke blown in my face, yet I was surprised with the solace it provided.

Within the first hour, I found myself sweating one moment and then very chilled the next. It felt as if a war were going on inside my body. My gut kept roaring and growling. I sensed I was losing strength in my arms and lay down on the floor. My body convulsed from time to time. Then I lost the ability to use my arms and legs; it was as if I were paralyzed. Throughout the night I had no fear, trusting the process and the presence of the shaman. It wasn't until daybreak that I could stand up, and I required support to walk.

Much of the ceremony must be kept private. Yes, unusual and scary things happened for most of the participants. Because the ceremony was sacred, I believe what was overheard and what was later described were deeply personal and merit privacy. What I can say about my own experience is that, aside from being very tired the next morning, I had no personal revelations, perhaps because I went into the ceremony with few needs, few intentions. I simply wanted time with the mother plant.

I attended three more ceremonies over the next few days, using different brews from different shamans, including Don Lucho, Don Enrique, and Don Wilma. There was also a slightly suspicious *tobaquero* shaman who was familiar with the tobacco plant *Nicotiana rustica*. With his entourage of adoring women, though, and because he didn't display the same trustworthiness and humility evinced by the other shamans, I chose not to be involved in his ceremony. Comparatively, I suspected that present in him was a dark element (*brujeria*)—the self-serving side of shamanism. I expressed my desire to keep a safe distance from his energy, even though I was just a plant-medicine gringo, and Carlos tacitly appeared to understand and respect my concern.

Chris's Hearing

My intrepid traveling companion, Chris, had given me permission to describe his hearing problem with one of our most trusted shaman guides, Don Enrique. Repeatedly, Chris asked other healers if aya could help restore hearing. He described, with great frustration and discouragement, the lack of progress he had made following extensive audiology consultations in Iowa and was more than eager to hear legitimate-sounding words of encouragement. Don Enrique satisfied that need.

Chris's hearing had steadily declined over a long period of time. He had purchased a very large-screen TV for his living room. An avid movie buff, Chris, along with his wife, had noticed that he had continuously adjusted the volume upward over the span of months, maybe years. He recalled that when the volume was set at forty-three, he could hear almost everything. His wife much preferred the volume at about twenty. The blasting sounds of the TV often were annoying for anyone in the same room with Chris. Understandably, he didn't like attention being called to his impairment.

Don Enrique offered to prepare a liquid concoction that he promised would help. As traditional healers know, any medicine will work better when a patient believes in it and in the healer's abilities, especially when the shaman exudes a similar confidence based on stories of his experience using selected plants. Chris expressed his emotional "buy in." Hope was elevated. Chris's mood rose—another harbinger for internal healing. Expectations were now set.

It took two days to locate, harvest, and blend all the plant medicines necessary for Chris's unique remedy. He eagerly awaited Don Enrique's return to camp each day, trusting that once the brew was in hand, and when it comingled with ayahuasca in his body, his hearing would improve. And then on the day of the treatment, he arrived with his customary soft smile.

In the jungle, liquid medicines are commonly delivered in used containers. Don Enrique gave Chris a two-liter Fanta soda bottle filled with a visually unappealing green liquid, advising him to drink it straight from the bottle over a designated period of time. Don Enrique brought more medicine to the camp just before our departure for the United States. Of course, we wondered if customs would discover it and dispassionately dump it, not knowing or appreciating the ingredients or their importance to Chris. But the medicine found its way home, and a second large bottle was ingested. What was initially a very unpleasant taste for Chris was becoming somewhat tolerable and banal. Each swig constituted a dose of hope.

And Don Enrique did not forget Chris even after his departure from Peru. The shaman continued to gather plant medicines, patiently extracting liquid from them, rendering a potent and absorbable remedy. Shortly after Chris had returned to the States from Iquitos, a UPS truck arrived with a parcel containing still more medicine, the amount needed to complete the recommended treatment regimen.

Less than a month had transpired when Chris noted that he was steadily adjusting his television volume setting downward. He had moved from the old setting of forty-three to twenty-two. Feeling relieved and curious, he scheduled a visit with his local physician and audiologist. Upon examining his ears, the doctor was a bit bemused, but pleased. A reconfiguration of the eardrum had occurred, something the doctor couldn't explain.

The physician asked, "Your ears look great; what have you been doing? That's the best they have ever looked. Your ear used to be conical shaped, now it isn't. The ear has changed *physically*! Whatever you are doing, keep it up."

When Chris pressed him for more details, his physician said, "The wall of your [one] ear was sucked in like a collapsed balloon and almost sitting on the eardrum, and now it isn't."

Chris revealed that he was treating himself with jungle-plant medicines. Unlike many doctors who would prefer to take full credit for a patient's recovery, the audiologist simply shared Chris's joy that significant physical changes had occurred and that some improvement in hearing was occurring.

Years later, I can report that Chris is still enjoying music and conversation at an improved level, but he wants to return for a booster dose.

A Healing Bath

During my trip to the Amazon with Chris, while I was walking around our jungle camp in the intense heat and humidity I usually wore only shorts and sandals. In my peripheral vision, one day I noticed one of the female shamans, Don Wilma, standing in the distance. She was conversing with two of her assistants—all of them, from time to time, glancing furtively in my direction. Eventually, someone approached me to convey their concerns.

It turns out that they had been noting three open sores on my back and surmised that I might have skin cancer. I had become so used to the presence of these sores, with all their bleeding and drainage, that it never dawned on me to solicit a shaman's opinion. Back home, I had seen three dermatologists over eighteen months, but there had been no improvements even after a number of treatments. My first doctor, in what seemed like primitive medicine, bent a razor blade into a U-shape and cut out deep samples to capture what was thought to be basal cell carcinoma and then sent them away for a biopsy. I was told to return for the results in a week but didn't, feeling that the diagnostic procedure had been crude (even though it is actually quite normal). The doctor wrote me a very stern letter, saying the equivalent of "get the hell in here, this could become more serious." Given his lack of tact, I chose not to return at all, trusting that my body would heal itself. Not so!

Months later, my dermatologist had moved on and another physician—a young woman fresh out of medical school—had taken over his practice. She, too, reached out, but this time in proper ethical fashion, and I did schedule an appointment. Several prescription treatments were attempted with no immediate results.

At that time, I was preparing to move from the mountains of Wyoming to the plains of Iowa. Consequently, with all the packing, unpacking, and obligations of setting up a new psychotherapy practice, finding another dermatologist was delayed. I was repeatedly flying between the two states and once, upon disembarking, I recall that a passenger to my rear asked, "Do you know you are bleeding? Your shirt is stained with blood."

I looked at the seatback and saw that I had left my mark. That was enough for me to schedule an appointment with a third dermatologist. He prescribed a strong topical ointment (Fluorouracil) that would likely begin an overdue healing process after a year-and-a-half delay. It, too, didn't work, despite repeated applications. I didn't pack the ointment for the trip.

At the Peruvian Amazon camp, Don Wilma and the other women offered to perform a bathing ritual for me, soaking me in a floral plant blend that they were confident would resolve my medical problem. Frankly, I was skeptical and dismissive, but I agreed to participate, despite my doubts, almost as an anthropological experiment. It is somewhat difficult for me to admit to my slightly duplicitous nature, but that is who I was in 2010. So, there I squatted in a large tin tub, flower pedals floating around my ankles, as three women repeatedly daubed me with the liquid medicine. In the oppressive heat of the jungle, the relief the bath afforded was enjoyable. But almost as soon as it concluded, my mind was on to other matters, such as the next aya ceremony. It, too, proved to be interesting, but it did not feel like a life-altering experience. Then, after ten adventurous but not necessarily eye-opening days in the jungle, I was back home.

Upon returning, there were bags to unpack, clothes to launder, and memories to retrieve and document. But before doing anything else, I elected to have a long, long shower. In the jungle, the opportunity to clean up was never very satisfying. Cool water was the norm. Now I could luxuriate in unlimited hot water. Preparing for my shower, I shed my shirt in front of some mirrors and turned to walk away. I caught a partial glance of my back. It stopped me in my tracks! I twisted and contorted my body better to examine myself and then grabbed a hand mirror for a closer look. Nothing was amiss! There were no sores! Just smooth, clean skin, as if there had never been an issue. A sudden and dramatic healing had occurred! Not surprisingly, the skeptic in me went for the programmed conclusion: my Western meds had coincidentally kicked in while I was on the trip.

In hindsight, it is hard for me to explain the rapid shift in my skin condition in the Amazon. While there, I had slept in an unclean bed. My body had been covered with sweat and dirt each day; I had been exposed to unsanitary eating conditions, and vermin were scampering about everywhere. Nevertheless, my recovery occurred and cannot be denied. Was it the ingredients of the bath, the aya, or some combination of healing factors? Maybe it was due simply to the passage of time; the healing just serendipitously occurred while I was in Peru. I may never know.

What I am certain of, though, is that whenever I have seen dramatic recoveries in indigenous communities, several elements have always been present: an atmosphere of expectant possibilities, a degree of mystery, and a cadre of supportive friends or caregivers surrounding the patients. Instead of limiting the source of indigenous (or my own) healing to supernatural powers, I prefer to think of it as the *super* natural power that can be awakened in all of us, especially when we are consistently planted on the skin of Pachamama. Jungle medicine is a very sophisticated way to tap the placebo in everyone who believes we are created with an innate, self-healing roadmap. It *is* a science, even though much of it is still not understood by the conscious mind but is rather a wisdom known to the subterranean "intellect," the unconscious. I also regard this ancient medicine as a form of sacred magic alive, although often unseen, in the universe. My ultimate nature is that of a human being who reverberates with the energy and wisdom of Mother Nature. Recognizing that my true identity goes far beyond the confines of my skin, I now stand in awe of this jungle medicine. It is a reminder of my connection to all life energies.

Traditional healers have helped me to locate myself in this interconnected web of life. The great mythologist and anthropologist Joseph Campbell said, "Today, the planet is the only proper 'in group.'" The Lakota people put this recognition in another way: *mitakuye oyasin,* meaning "all my relatives." This awareness, in contrast to thoughts of isolation, is life sustaining. It makes loneliness seem like a delusion, an impossibility. And the web connecting all life forms is the doctor.

Ojibwa Healing of
Interpersonal Violence

On the last day of a vacation in Nova Scotia, I visited a shopping mall in search of a bookstore. My flight home would afford me a lot of free time, so a good book would be nice. With six new books stacked in arm, I headed to the checkout. There I noticed a display featuring a new book, *Returning to the Teachings*, by Rupert Ross. About aboriginal justice, it recounts how a Canadian Ojibwa tribe had infused a broken legal system with sacred tribal teachings and rediscovered the healing powers of their old ways. By the time I noticed it, I had already selected more than enough books, paid for my treasure trove, and left the store. Plopped down on a mall bench facing the bookstore, I kept noticing the same display.

As an insatiable bibliophile struggling to show restraint, I responsibly said to myself, "It's time to quit for the day. Enough." Then the rationalizing part of me took over, saying, "You know you are going to buy it, so just get it over with." Back into the store I went and added Rupert's book to my collection. That event in 1997 eventually proved deeply transformative.

After years as a psychotherapist specializing in interpersonal violence, by the time I read Rupert's book I had spent a significant amount of my professional time in courtrooms, imagining, as the biblical figure Amos proclaimed, that "righteousness and justice would roll down like a mighty stream" (Amos 5:24). I had long believed that healing could occur in courtrooms; just as the Roman statue of Lady Justice implies, balance and harmony will prevail. Despite constant examples to the contrary, and witnessing emotional pain exacerbated by our legal system, I remained loyal to my illusion that laws, attorneys, and judges created portals to personal restoration following abuse and exploitation. I marched in step with the masses who subscribed to the old notion that when laws were broken and charges were brought against obvious perpetrators, a guilty verdict would expedite healing, certainly not open more wounds.

Rupert, on the other hand, as a Crown attorney in northwest Ontario, had witnessed his notions of justice eroding year after year. He was filled with despair for everyone, including the prosecutor. Family members were paraded in and out of courtrooms after hurts, betrayals, and abuses—nearly all of them total strangers to the court, the majority of them Ojibwa. Always the answer to domestic or sexual abuse involved the application of white legal and psychological remedies, few of which ever made a dent in the underlying precipitants to crime. Rupert realized that individual and community healing had to involve ministering to fractured relationships, not just broken laws. Jailing someone merely postponed, or totally avoided, any kind of restorative justice. Fining a poverty-stricken individual, and giving the proceeds to the government, never repaired a single emotional wound.

These methods just created a ritually embedded and deceptively simple mask of what justice purported to be.

In *Returning to the Teachings,* Rupert cited the wisdom to which he had been exposed by the elder women of one remote tribe, Hollow Water First Nation of neighboring Manitoba, outlining their stories of sacred, satisfying, and restorative justice. This was how I first learned of that Ojibwa community, my subsequent trips to which I have recounted earlier. By the time my series of flights was finished from Halifax to Sheridan, Wyoming, I had finished Rupert's book, underlined and highlighted key parts, and created my own index so that I could quickly locate poignant passages. It had made an impression.

After a couple of days, I was on the phone to Penguin Books in Toronto asking how I might locate and communicate with Rupert. I was provided a phone number. And to my surprise, Rupert himself picked up the phone in his kitchen while preparing supper and kindly delayed his meal to speak with me. I told him it would be grand if I could visit the Hollow Water community, and sensing my sincerity, he quickly committed to making that possible.

A few months later, I was in eastern Manitoba, meeting with one of the central founding figures in the tribe's healing initiatives, Burma Bushie. Not long afterward, I sat down personally with Rupert. He fast became a cherished friend, and our relationship lives on. Since the late 1990s, I have returned to Hollow Water many times to watch the tribe's program evolve—and at times devolve, with waxing and waning community interest. Nevertheless, their model of healing from interpersonal abuse is solid, and I intend to keep its principles alive in every article and book I write on mending the wounds of fractured relationships. What follows is my interpretation of their core principles.

Having been trained in traditional psychology, I have now served as a healer and an educator for forty-five years, witnessing astonishing transformations in the emotional and physical healing of many patients who have suffered in the aftermath of physical and sexual abuse. As satisfying as it has been to accompany individuals on their healing paths, I have always thought that something seemed to be missing from the process. The rigidity of my university-trained, psychological model felt limiting and unnatural to me. It wasn't heartfelt and responsive, and it was without the reverence for which victims and abusers yearned to help them heal on a deep level. Psychologists seem to walk in lockstep with our Diagnostic and Statistical Manual of Mental Disorders (DSM-5) in hand and respond to patients with one-size-fits-all treatment protocols, a "disease" of sorts that I have come to call *hardening of the categories*. At the same time, I was opening to complementary or alternate paradigms, new and/or old, that could incorporate sacred principles into the mix.

Upon meeting with Ojibwa medicine people, a spirit-driven model began to minister to my best essence and opened doors to a more sanctified approach to patient care. The Ojibwas also showed me that victims of abuse can not only retrieve their basic essence following a soul loss, but they also can do far more than cope and survive; many have not just bounced back after adversity, they have bounced forward. As opposed to the model of chronic breakage coined posttraumatic stress disorder (PTSD), when treatment included culturally familiar sacred approaches, an ensuing process of posttraumatic growth could easily ensue.

Being with victims and abusers in sacred circles of support has convinced me that the basis of any meaningful change must be a personally meaningful spiritual foundation. Once again, we can't ignore patient-belief systems while imposing our own culture's ideas on other people. That is especially important when patients are from, or embedded in, a culture fundamentally different from our own. More than in modern Western culture, indigenous peoples place far more emphasis on *relational* approaches, recognizing that abuses rarely develop in a vacuum and are rarely healed in a one-on-one office setting with a stranger. As an indigenous informed caregiver walks the Healing Path with patients while honoring their interconnected worldview, the caregiver can also undergo a wonderful meta-morphosis. By bearing witness as the patients overcome their darkness, we are challenged to be at least equally courageous in addressing our own personal wounds. Sitting in circle with wounded persons can, as Dr. Martin Luther King Jr. suggested, become a double victory.[1]

The Hollow Water Epidemic of Sexual Abuse

For decades, the Western world, particularly the United States and Canada, went through an epidemic of sexual abuse that now, fortunately, is experiencing a steep decline. Perhaps we are doing something right, maybe in our counseling offices or as a result of our public-health educational programs. The same results, however, were not being seen in Hollow Water, or other Native communities, as the psyches of aboriginal people were not responsive to the imposition of our beliefs and methodologies. When I first visited Hollow Water mental-health workers in 1997, I naively inquired of them just how common sexual abuse was on their reserve. Speaking with a predominantly female group, I asked for an estimate of the percentage of women who were victims of sexual assault. After some silence, and noting the perplexed looks on their faces, it dawned on me that my query was fundamentally flawed. Eventually, I learned that virtually every female member of this Ojibwa tribe had been abused, often many times, long before reaching adulthood. A better question on my part might have been whether they knew of anyone who was *not* the victim of chronic childhood maltreatment.

Sexual abuse was linked to the tribe's pervasive problem of addiction to drugs, alcohol, and sex. It was also linked to the governing male power structure within the tribe. There was also the undeniable intergenerational impact of colonization, whereby people who have experienced chronic trauma within the context of exploitation by an oppressor—whether that be a government or a church—lose the meaning of themselves, their purpose, and even their cultural affiliation. The very structure of the self—one's values and ideals—is systematically broken down. The childrens' most tangible trauma may come from sexual abuse by Catholic priests, but it is exacerbated by being forced to live far from their nuclear families in residential schools, forbidden to speak in their native tongue, denied to dress in any way suggesting individualism, and being punished and shamed for practicing cultural activities. The result is a deleterious sense of soul loss or soul theft and disabling despondency that, along with the accompanying sense of disempowerment, can be tacitly passed forward for generations.

The Imposition of White Solutions

Outsiders—police officials, social workers, psychologists, attorneys, and judges—descended on this tiny and remote village of six hundred Ojibwas, confidently applying solutions for the problem of sexual abuse that were often sincerely intended to be remedial but that were designed for distant people living under fundamentally different circumstances. The Royal Canadian Mounted Police (Mounties) investigated the "crimes" and gathered evidence for criminal prosecution, while the Crown recommended incarceration and the pilfering of the abuser's money that could have more appropriately stayed within the family and supported the victims. Task completed, on to the next case!

Upon conviction, abusers were quickly and routinely sent to a prison in the southern part of the province, what women of the tribe called the "Holiday Inn of the South." This was a place where prisoners drank coffee, watched television, played cards, looked at pornography, and masturbated while free meals were provided for them.

What nonsense! the women declared. Prisons were just an escape from daily responsibilities, a vacation from the tensions on the reserve. Little, if any, reflection and soul searching would take place there. Far from Hollow Water, the abusers were under no pressure to review the pain they had inflicted. They had no opportunity to dialogue with victims in a respectful way, nor any sense of duty instilled to contribute to the restorative healing of the victims and the ruptures in the community they had caused. And then soon the abusers were back home again, where they resumed their reign of terror, living out their unhealed wounds from long ago, subconsciously trying to turn their tragedy narrative into what felt like a triumph.

Women of the tribe came to decry the dangers of incarceration. Prison sentences dropped men into a culture of denial, while removing them from their spiritual roots and the wise ways of the elders. Incarceration offered no solutions; in fact, it perpetuated crime. Not allowing victim-offender dialogue in the court proceedings relegated both parties to the role of spectators of their own lives.

A Canadian flag was always displayed in the often-makeshift courtrooms. *But where was the eagle staff?* the women wondered. And why was the process so rushed before the community could even attempt an intervention? If only there were a way to slow down the legal process and not get swept up in its momentum of irrelevancy, which was the opposite complaint to that usually heard in the dominant Canadian culture and in the United States.

The Proclamation

After years of being beaten down physically and psychologically by a number of forces, a group of women convened meetings and prepared to speak out. They would speak the words bearing their shame: *sexual abuse.* Their resolve was strong, and male tribal officials, most of whom had been involved in some form of sexual abuse as adults, were put on notice that dialogue was about to begin.

The women's guiding principles were printed and disseminated in the form of a position paper. It was a declaration of independence from oppression, while at the same time a declaration of tribal interdependence. This was not a throwaway culture in which women were used as sexual objects and discarded. Nor was it a culture that threw away its long-damaged men while calling it a solution. The women realized that the true cause of sexual abuse stemmed from the loss of tribal identity and the spiritual traditions that once formed a strong bond among community members. To pursue vengeance or punishment, they wrote, only kept the abuser's spirit alive in their own hearts, thereby impeding their own healing. If their individual and collective souls were to be retrieved, it would require a new/old way of being. This could occur only with a return to their sacred roots, when the norm had been not retributive justice but restorative justice circles of healing.

Historically, the Ojibwa relied on active dialogue to resolve conflicts, often while sitting in a circle for many hours until understanding and consensus were reached. No adversarial talking through attorneys who sat at separate tables facing a judge and the Canadian flag! A cleansing smudge, prayer, sweat lodge, community feasting, proper placement of the eagle staff, elder storytelling—all of these activities were employed to foster a return to harmony. And, ideally, such activities would occur at a sacred location or in a sacred setting. Face-to-face conversation, guided by respectful values, was the traditional way delicate matters were resolved. A talking piece—perhaps a feather, a stone, or an object of great personal meaning—was passed from person to person. You spoke when it was your turn; you listened attentively when the talking piece was in the hands of someone else. Rituals were practiced as part of an overarching ceremony, while both parties were surrounded by their own network of community supporters that included friends, relatives, and occasionally strangers. But always a dignified decorum created a safe place. To harm any one person was the equivalent of harming the entire community; you couldn't be separated from the larger family.

Putting Form to Ideas

Reflecting back on their ancient tribal traditions, the women of Hollow Water realized that sexual abuse was not an individual crime as much as it was the symptom of an entire community that had drifted away from its sacred, organizing practices. They had fallen out of balance with each other and with the interwoven forms of life seen throughout Nature. Community self-examination was as important as any one person's admission of guilt and apology. Each crime was a wake-up call reminding everyone of the importance of tribal mental health.

A shift in healing practices would have to include the revitalization of spiritual ceremonies that had been stolen by the dominant culture. Healing of interpersonal conflicts would include movement away from unsuccessful legalistic attempts that fashioned crime as a violation of provincial statutes—a very detached way of looking at harm. With amazing cooperation from the Crown and federal judges, the legal system began listening and showed a willingness to bend. The courts were presented with the women's position paper in which they clearly asserted that courtrooms were unsafe places for victims and abusers. Incarceration, they contended, offered no healing for abusers and only provided time for perpetrators of harm to entrench themselves in the collective denial fostered among prison inmates. They came home worse than before.

Further, no longer would it be deemed acceptable for abusers to be banished from the community. Jails and prisons, the women argued, should rarely be used, except with only the most recalcitrant and uncooperative abusers. Both courtrooms and prisons were to be avoided whenever it was safely feasible.

Sexual abuse was too serious a problem to be handled in those unresponsive settings.

Nearly all abusers, the women contended, should be required to stay at Hollow Water for an extended period of time before court proceedings commenced. Immediately, each person involved, whether victim or perpetrator, was directed to a *circle of support*—one for the victim, one for the abuser—to begin a restorative dialogue with community members. Traditional rituals would provide a scaffolding to support sacred space and reduce risk of further harm. The women went a step further. In the event that the court became involved in a case, they asked the Crown ultimately to support community-sentencing circles in which each tribal member could come forward and offer a solution; the judge and attorneys being relegated to the task of gathering consensus and fashioning it into an order.

The women also proposed that before any court proceeding on First Nation land, a number of Ojibwa rituals needed to be respectfully employed. Before any court activity, a community feast would occur with everyone being invited, including the Royal Canadian Mounted Police, attorneys, judges, and all tribal members, together with victims and those persons accused of abuse. This constituted the coming together of all people, which set the tone for what followed. Anyone having been to prison before was welcome.

Following the sharing of food, a medicine person would make a tobacco offering and smudge the courtroom inside and out. The tribe's eagle-feather staff (a symbol comparable to our flag, making a statement about their identity in Nature), a ceremonial drum, and the Canadian flag would be cleansed as well. Then all these important symbols of each culture would be placed with equal respect on the floor, in the center of the circle where sacred business would convene. At the same time, though, the superiority or power the symbols represented was understood to be diminished in this courtroom. Even the judge, along with the flag, would come down from his elevated platform to join the circle at the same level as the eagle staff, the drum, and all the participants. And once attorneys had had their time to speak, they were disallowed the chance to jump up to object and interrupt the ritualized proceeding.

A prayer would signal that the hearing was now in session. No matter how many people requested to speak, everyone would eventually receive the talking piece (in some rare cases an actual microphone), with no attorney jumping up to clamor, "Objection, Your Honor!" Whoever didn't have the talking piece would remain sitting and silent, awaiting their turn.

And when it was time for sentencing, the rituals would begin anew, with everyone again eventually having an opportunity to hold the talking piece, no matter how many people wanted to speak. A sentencing ceremony could take as many as twelve hours to complete. There would be no rush to justice.

Thus, with the authorities signing on, something sacred would begin to transpire in the once dangerously adversarial courtroom. Victims' voices were being heard again and, in the process, there were soul retrievals. Hardly anyone was being sent to jail or prison.

The astonishing result is that some of the abusers did so well in the firm embrace of their community that they took on new roles. No longer were they just criminal perpetrators; some were even encouraged to assume the role of healers, joining forces with their former counselors to help others similarly charged with abuse—including women. Again, everyone was placed on an equal footing; gender took a back seat to the human task at hand. Both sexes could join ranks in the effort of healing, unlike in most Western group-therapy sessions. I once witnessed a sexual abusers' group that welcomed a female assailant in the circle. While admittedly this is a rare practice, I did see it happen. They really were thinking out of the box, if not blowing up the box altogether.

So, does the approach of replacing the standard courtroom with traditional communal ceremonies really work? Federal research into the Manitoba experiment determined that not only was this method more cost effective, but it also significantly lowered the rate of recidivism from crimes of interpersonal violence.

Personal Challenges; Busting Paradigms

Trained in psychology as I was, with decades of experience working with sexual abusers, their victims, and families, I realized that the Ojibwa approach offered many missing pieces to my therapeutic paradigm. In addition, my experiences at Hollow Water inspired me to be a better healer—and a better person too. I became more deeply committed to my own healing path and far less ego driven and focused on financial success. I, too, recognized my part in the community in which I healed patients, but not from an elevated level of personal importance, and not so much an expert as a collaborator.

One winter evening, while I was sitting outdoors with a medicine man, he asked a series of probing, and usually rhetorical, questions about my profession. Through questions and storytelling, he politely but firmly nudged me to grow a bit.

For example, he asked, "What is that bible you psychologists use, you know, the one used to call people names?" Of course, he was referring to the DSM, which has words only to diagnose diseases, disorders, and dysfunctions without any diagnostic terminology that suggests that a person can also be resilient and have many positive qualities and character strengths that hold the potential for personal transformation.

"Doesn't dissing people *freeze* people?" the medicine man further inquired, suggesting that to be known only by their assigned diagnostic label locks people into an entrenched identity. He went on to say, "We don't let our children call each other names; as elders we must set an example for them." He reminded me that Native people of the North are often assigned new names as they undergo life challenges, return from fasts, come home from military service, or are seen in other new ways.

Next, he asked, "Why is it that you put so many of your people in cages? I did that to one of my dogs after neighbors feared he might bite someone. He was very gentle, but he lived in a cage for one year before I felt so bad that I released him. Then, suddenly and for the first time, he bit me! So, how does caging heal your people?"

I knew enough not to answer; my obligation was to be a respectful listener in the company of an elder's wisdom.

After some reflective quiet time, the old man, in a seemingly innocent voice, asked a couple more powerful questions: "Why is it that you take money from injured people for the privilege of being able to walk with them on their Healing Path? Haven't they been hurt enough?"

Nothing more needed to be said; the questions had their answers embedded within them.

The Healing Path

In Ojibwa culture, there is an understanding that people heal best when in the company of others. Sexual abusers are encouraged and supported by the entire community to walk on a Healing Path. It matters not so much where they are on that path; what is important is that they are moving on a better path than their previous one. In their Anishinaabe language, there is a paucity of nouns but plenty of verbs. People are always moving, growing, evolving, changing, and so on. They don't remain stuck in nouns such as *criminal*, *pervert*, *sex offender*, or *psychopath*. As my friend Rupert Ross often says in response to this way of speaking, "To noun, noun, noun me is to no, no, no me."[2]

I find the Ojibwa cosmology comparable to the Navajo conceptualization of the Pollen Path. It is a never-ending journey that seeks balance, harmony, and connection with all of Mother Earth's creations. The understanding is that disharmony causes illnesses—physical and emotional. A return to harmony is what heals, more than any plant medicine or medical procedure.

As Rupert writes, "Aboriginal healing processes constantly stress values such as respect, sharing, humility, and so forth. It has to do with an understanding that the Healing Path is not something 'sick' people need, totally 'healthy' people supervise, and the rest of us can largely ignore. It is a path we must all walk on. We all have healing contributions to make to others along the path, and others have healing contributions to make to us."[3]

In Ojibwa culture, little separation exists among healers and abusers as everyone is thought to be in the process of becoming a better person—a changed person. This dynamic is evident in the case of a man named Richard, whom I met during one of my many visits to Hollow Water. Richard was a recovering alcoholic who had raped his daughters; beaten his wife; assaulted community members, including a counselor and a police officer; and ignited the family home with three of his children inside it during a rage-filled moment fueled by alcohol. Fortunately, no one died in the blaze.

From my perspective as a psychologist, Richard could easily have met the diagnostic criteria of a psychopath. To my astonishment, following a lengthy intervention period and a twelve-hour community sentencing during which no one recommended incarceration, Richard remained free. Now, he no longer drinks, and he is no longer violent.

At his sentencing hearing, it had been determined that Richard had fallen out of contact with other community members. The Ojibwa believe that this kind of isolation is what leads to crime. Accordingly, the community was ordered to visit with him more regularly, to play cards with him, and to honk and wave as they saw him walking with his head down on the roadway—all in an effort to bring him back into the community's gaze and embrace.

A criminal, the Hollow Water Ojibwa believe, is someone who acts as if he has no relatives. The response is to summon the relatives, whether blood related or not, including ancestors who have passed or animals with special powers. Central to Richard's restoration was a resumption of his participation in traditional ceremonies, including the sweat lodge and joining the community on its annual Black Island Day celebration.

He was not, however, extended the privilege of escaping to prison. Since Richard was a fisherman, one person suggested that a consequence of his behavior would be to donate walleye pike to elders in the community. Not only would such gifts emphasize generosity and reciprocity—key Ojibwa values—but they would also result in many doors being opened to him with smiling faces. By not being banished from the tribe, Richard was forced to explore the damage created by his actions, to listen to his daughters again and again, to make amends, and to attend counseling. Destructive shaming by community members was not allowed, as it serves no healing purpose.

Individuals such as Richard have encouraged me to reach deeply into my soul, my essence. Previously I struggled, with great difficulty, to rediscover my human capacity to feel and express compassion for all people, even for those whose ways I didn't like. With the gifts received from Hollow Water, I now can see the difference between liking and loving people—the latter being my job and the easier of the two. I recognize that wounded people hurt other people in turn. This requires me to see everyone's wounds and minister to them, even when I don't like their ways. It requires me to treat abusers lovingly with support, respect, and dignity, thereby keeping the best part of myself alive. The other goal in walking this path is to model—and hopefully develop—a compassionate side in the abuser.

Lessons from Hollow Water

Today, I view aboriginal healing methods as part of a sacred obligation to my community, as well as a personal gift that allows me the opportunity momentarily to immerse myself in human darkness, where it is the easiest to see a ray of light. As a result of my days with the wise and loving people of Hollow Water, I have learned an invaluable lesson. Restorative justice healing is a community engagement, one that leaves every participant changed. We are one, impacted and molded by the intentions and activities of all our brothers and sisters. It is an inescapable web of connectivity.

Ancient healing methods are reemerging on every continent, addressing a wide range of social and emotional issues, from shoplifting to murder. Following the examples of traditional medicine women and men, we are once again learning that it is not people's rap sheets but their evolving relationships that are most important—relationships with one another, with the physical environment, and with the Creator and all her creations. Ojibwa healing is *relational* healing—how the grass relates to the wind, how the water responds to Grandmother Moon, and how we love each other.

Individuals are at their strongest when their ego lessens its stranglehold and relational ties with others grow. In the Anishinaabe language, *ain-dah-ing* refers to the Seventh Direction, going inward. It is *mash-ka-wisen,* the place where the heart and soul reside. As I have roughly interpreted these words, they mean, "Return to your heart for healing." That is where the healing happens.

Strength can arise after being harshly tested. As an old Quaker woman once said to me, "People are like teabags; you don't know how strong they will become until they are dipped in some hot water." Such strength often follows traumatic experiences in the North Window of our lives. This North Window is associated with the white buffalo that, undaunted, stares down bitter storms, unlike other animals that turn their rears to life's challenges. The North Window of our lives is a time for mentoring, when we finally understand the lessons of life's vicissitudes and, with that understanding, discover the duty to mentor the younger generation who is following us. For all the knowledge that comes from suffering, we are encouraged by Ojibwa philosophy to maintain a grateful heart.

The Anishinaabe word for this appreciation is *megwetch*, which translates to "thank you." There is the notion that thanks should be extended to Creator for all the teachings received, whether they are deemed good, bad, or ugly, as everything can be transformed into a positive if faced in the right way. For that example, I say megwetch!

Ojibwa Restorative Justice Compared to Western Law

Aboriginal healing traditions, as witnessed in Hollow Water, stand in stark contrast to contemporary court proceedings. The former is profoundly sensitive, the other coldly mechanistic; one is cooperative, the other encourages further conflict and injury, as detailed in the below chart.

WESTERN LEGAL SYSTEM	OJIBWA RESTORATIVE JUSTICE
Focuses on criminal acts and broken laws	Focuses on broken relationships
Seeks punishment and vengeance	Teaches, reconnects, supports, and restores
Incarcerates before and after sentencing	Avoids banishment and isolation
Fines people; proceeds go to the government	Encourages reparations and relational amends to victims
Requires a judge or jury to hear the case	Encourages community sentencing
Pushes for a finding of guilt	Delays proceedings until guilt is acknowledged and treatment is underway
Applies criminal labels upon conviction	Avoids "nouning" a person, which can undermine growth and discourage change
Denies most prisoners meaningful treatment in jail	Immediately offers abusers and victim community-based healing
Allows pretrial motions, bargaining, bluffing	Relies on transparency in circles and rituals
Rushes to adjudicate and remove abuser from society	Avoids court and incarceration whenever possible
Punishes law violations	Teaches community duties and responsibilities
Focuses entirely on postcrime matters	Emphasizes prevention and restoration using sacred practices
Employs (masculine) hierarchical structure	Applies (feminine) circular model, shared participation
Orders individual counseling in clinics	Encourages community-based, spiritual recovery ceremonies in Nature

TABLE 1. Two Diverse Systems of Accountability. (Copyright by the author)

Grizzly Bear
Medicine

Few animals evoke more trepidation and even terror than the brown bears, particularly the *ursus arctos horribilis,* the North American grizzly bear. Having lived in northern Wyoming for a quarter century, I've spent countless weekends in the mountains near Yellowstone National Park watching and photographing the grizzly. Even though I have been just a few yards from this magnificent animal, and while I respect its astonishing power, never have I had a threatening encounter. I was the exception, however, as many fellow residents of the Cowboy State have been charged and mauled by Grizz.

While I have long been fascinated by the circumstances that precipitated such occurrences—usually a bear was startled in its day bed, or a hiker got between a mother and her cubs—the bear was, more often than not, simply establishing physical boundaries. Rather than seek to kill and eat humans, Grizz are almost always telling us, in their sudden and blunt ways, to be more polite in their homeland. They would rather neutralize a perceived threat than draw blood. And even when someone is viciously mauled, the bear will eventually retreat and not eat the remains. Don't get me wrong: they love raw meat, but they would much rather munch on an elk or a black angus than swallow human flesh.

Trained in psychology and trauma resolution, I have always been intrigued about the behavior of survivors of grizzly mauling. Once an attack is over and the victim is sewn back together, the nature lovers would return to the forest soon thereafter. Amazingly, most had no animosity toward the bear. They knew it was their mistake that caused the bear to unleash its defensive wrath, regarded it impersonally as just a fact of Nature, and often resisted the game warden's efforts to euthanize the animal.

I spent one summer and fall interviewing regional survivors of brutal bear attacks, compiling their stories in my book, *Grizzly Lessons: Coexisting with Bears and Wolves*. Some were permanently disfigured—an eye missing or a face scarred—but, by and large, life went on. Only once did I encounter an individual who was diagnosed with PTSD because of an attack.

This general absence of PTSD among bear-attack survivors contrasted vividly with my psychotherapy practice, in which other agencies referred patients to me carrying the PTSD diagnosis, frequently after a divorce, being fondled by a relative, or perhaps a chronic barrage of verbal abuse. I also noted that many indigenous cultures were unfamiliar with a PTSD diagnosis, and, without it, their members did not stay frozen in terror following a tragic and painful life experience. I learned that what mattered wasn't the event so much as it was how people *responded* to the event.

In the Western United States, Native Americans have long revered, and many times feared, the noble animal known as the grizzly. They have a unique view of Grizz. He is regarded as a close relative and the bringer of medicine. So, what started as a simple interest on my part evolved into a study of the brown bear's positive influence on Native people, especially in terms of their healing beliefs and methods.

Obstacles to Healing

The first order of business for every traditional healer, as well as every psychotherapist, is to remove every impediment before commencing a treatment, and fear is one of the major impediments to healing. It is one emotion that healers and psychotherapists routinely address, day in and day out. Their own fears must first be overcome if they are to become a potent medicine person. The patient brings fright, terror, and phobias of his or her own and will need a therapist who is solid and steady, someone who can model fearlessness and help shoulder their burdens.

Often the animal world instructs us on how to live more confidently and how to diminish our fears. The Grizz is a teacher of quiet, reserved strength, but he can either assuage dread or cause alarm, depending on how he is approached and understood. Simply seeing a grizzly close up puts us in touch with our fear; and, for a traditional healer, that is when important training commences. Learning how to be comfortable in the company of bears prepares us to stand next to patients with a steady and modest fearlessness. No emotion will unravel us. Our equanimity calms the troubled heart.

During the many years I have spent traveling throughout the world to study the medicine people of indigenous cultures, numerous animals have visited me, each with its own unique and sometimes confounding demeanor. Not long ago a silver-back gorilla approached me on a mountainside just inside the Democratic Republic of the Congo. I cautiously froze as this giant beauty brushed against me when it ambled by, seemingly indifferent to my presence. I was nervous but not afraid, and he himself showed no fear, although gorillas are regularly poached in the area. With each step, he grunted, and I matched his sounds while averting my gaze.

On another occasion in Tanzania, a striped hyena unrelentingly circled my pup tent for most of one evening. Eerie vocalizations reminded me of its constant presence, while I tried to determine how to address a persistent dysentery problem without jeopardizing my safety each time I was compelled to exit my tent quickly for relief.

Then there was the time in Zimbabwe when I was visiting traditional healers. Baboons rattled my cabin-door handle and later raced across the tin roof for much of the night. They were persistently searching for a way to break in, intimidate me, grab my food, and vamoose—at least that was the local shaman's explanation. All these events were unnerving yet exhilarating, too, just as encountering a Grizz in Wyoming or Montana would be. I worry about the day when I can longer experience wild adventures of this kind.

A Grizzly Encounter at Dawn

Once during a seemingly eternal dawn of Alaska's summertime, while hiking alone on the shore of the McNeil River, I witnessed a mysterious creature approaching me on its hind legs. It appeared half-human and half-animal, like the legendary depictions of the sasquatch of the North Woods. It slowly neared me, walking up the river on its hind legs. Its wet fur was tightly clinging to its side, creating the outline of what looked like a monstrous human. The low light, matched with my bright imagination, at first prevented me from properly identifying what kind of creature it was.

As the reader might expect, until I determined what was converging on me, fear kept ramping up with each step the creature took in my direction, until I finally realized that I was being approached by a large, Kodiak brown bear. Strangely, with that insight, my panic diminished. I suspect that over the years my familiarity with bears had had a calming effect, even though I understood their potential for defensive savagery.

I knew enough that day not to impede a bear. A polite person is generally safe in bear country. Along with my shaman friend in the Amazon, I know that some of us animals demand a certain amount of space for comfort. So, I averted my gaze and turned my body to the side to avoid signaling a frontal challenge. In a few moments he passed, and both of us were comfortably on our way.

The Revered Bear

While aboriginal people of North America have almost universally feared bears, they have simultaneously venerated Grizz. Many tribes regarded the grizzly as a medicine being or shaman to the animal world, the Apache contending that this awesome animal was the very first great shaman among all the relatives. Inuits (Eskimos) of the Canadian Arctic still carve stone depictions of shamans that are half-human and half-bear. My home is adorned with a few examples of their art. Native Americans consider bears to be the closest relative to humans in the animal kingdom, as well as a creature of strong healing abilities, but Grizz is the noblest of them all. Because of this, grizzlies are often sought after as guardian animals or spirit helpers.

FIGURE 8. Grizzly Bear. Also known as the North American brown bear, Grizz is commonly regarded as a spirit helper.

The shamans of many Native tribes of North America—the Assiniboin, Fox, Cree, Winnebago, and Zuni, to name a few— often shapeshifted into the demeanor of grizzly bears, imitating them in an attempt to assimilate some of the bear's potent healing wisdom and strength. This required living like, moving like, and thinking like Grizz: in essence, "dancing" bear qualities into their very being. To the extent that a medicine person or shaman could accurately mimic Grizz, it was believed that the senses of both animals could potentially be enjoined and the healer's perspective would likely be enhanced by the bear.

Shapeshifting offered a stereoscopic view of the world, one that could bind all beings—an experience rarely achieved by living a singular and isolated existence.

Midewiwin Medicine-Lodge Society

In my regular travels to Manitoba, Canada, I have participated in the Hollow Water First Nation's Ojibwa sweat-lodge ceremonies. In antiquity, their Midewiwin Medicine-Lodge Society, a secret alliance, held the bear as its patron supporter, and the spirit of the bear was often incorporated into healer initiation rituals during healing ceremonies. Today, some Ojibwa healers still apply wisdom from the Midewiwin Society. During a sweat-lodge purification ceremony, they may humbly crawl into the lodge on hands and knees, grunting like a bear, and, in so doing, invite the spirit of the bear to accompany them into the sweats. As in many other cultures sensitive to certain animals in their natural world, here it is about humbly imploring the animal's aid.

Some Native American medicine people will also encourage their patients to eat bear grease just as the healer does, in order for the healer to receive guidance in preparing a proper diagnosis and to perform a cure. Bear grease may also be rubbed on the site of an ailment to assist in the healing process. A bear talisman, perhaps a claw, may be worn during the ceremony to pay homage to this revered relative.

Ojibwa traditional language provides another clue as to how strong this affinity with the bear can be. Bears are referred to in their native tongue as *anijinabe*, the Anishinaabe word for "The People," identifying the bear as one of them.

Bear As Teacher and Healer

Careful observation of a bear's eating habits has long guided medicine people to healing plants believed to share their consciousness with humans, thereby becoming spiritual helpers. Both the animal and the plant can merge spirits as good medicine, and, interestingly, one word for "bear" in the Acoma Pueblo language is the same as their word for "medicine person" or "shaman."[1] Pueblo healers are said to have used bear root (also referred to as bear medicine or osha root) to transport individuals into a trance-like state, in which the cause of an illness could better be seen and treated.

Other tribes believed that as the result of ingesting part of the heart of a grizzly bear, great healing abilities would be bestowed onto them. The Tlingit of British Columbia, however, avoided the ingestion of anything bear, having a strict taboo about eating bear flesh because bears were regarded as being half-human and, therefore, close relatives. Eating bear was too close to cannibalism.

Becoming Bear

There are other lessons to be had from watching bears' behavior, particularly when they enter into their secluded, annual hibernation den and months later experience a springtime rebirth and renewal. A human example comes from the Arctic. I recall listening to the recent account of an Alaskan Inuit hunter named Morris, who, while riding his snowmobile alongside a friend, fell through the thin ice one bitterly cold day on a remote Alaskan lake, plunging into dangerously frigid water. Unable to make it to shore and to avoid drowning, Morris wisely wedged an arm into the steelwork of his machine so tightly that he would stay afloat and keep his face just above the water line even if he lost strength or became unconscious.

Recalling his family origins in the Bear Clan, Morris decided to hibernate, like his animal relatives do, and faded in and out of consciousness while awaiting the results of his trusted companion's walk for miles back to their home community in order to summon rescuers. For over three hours, Morris bobbed in the frigid water in subzero surface temperatures. He volitionally moved in and out of hibernation to check for any help that might be coming his way. When rescuers finally arrived, they boated out to him, pulled him onboard with his soaked clothing, and then put him in a pickup truck to transport him to the village where a plane would fly him to a hospital. Two more hours had passed after his rescue before he arrived at the hospital and was slowly warmed.

Having never been told by medical "authorities" that a person cannot survive beyond thirty minutes in icy water, Morris defied scientific knowledge. No medical problems were detected, no medical care was provided, and Morris was released the same day to go home.

As his doctor said, "He's no worse for the wear and I can't explain it."

Morris wasn't surprised by the outcome because bears never need veterinary care following hibernation, so how would he be any different? Bear's familiar example, and an open mind, saved him.

Later, Morris explained, "Water is cold only if you think it is cold. And my mind knew what to do; my body just tagged along."

Hibernating bears inform us of the importance of periodic retreats, entering into solitude for fasting, rest, and reflection but always returning to the world for reengagement, in a pattern much like Joseph Campbell's description of the hero's journey. This "dipping in and out" becomes a resurrection of sorts.

Transitional Rites and Grizzly Bear Therapy

Bears also provide hints of how initiation rites—disappearing into the forest for enlightenment in preparation for life's next transition—can be choreographed. For the Ojibwa, *Makwa Manido,* "Bear Spirit," provides a path for strengthening and renewal. Traditionally, a young girl at the arrival of her first *wemukowe,* her first menstruation, would be whisked away into the bush by an elder woman and left in a secluded hut. The girl, soon to be a woman, was said to be "going to be a bear" and upon her return to camp would be referred to as *mukowe,* literally translating to "she is now bear."

It is believed that great physical and spiritual powers are derived simply from being in the company of bears. This is of particular importance to indigenous people, because many tribes understand that humans are the only creatures in the world who are essentially helpless when born. We can, however, develop into stronger beings when in the company of our more powerful animal relatives. Humbly, we must rely on these close relatives to garner strength from their carefully observed example and their regular presence in our lives.

Some Native American cultures believe that when a person is approached by a bear, especially a grizzly, the animal can imbue that person with great restorative energy to be used on themselves and others. This energy has such a strong force that it can be difficult to contain once it resides in you. As is true of grizzlies, a person with this force must exercise restraint as a highly developed quality. When managed in a cautious and reverent manner, the energy can be transmitted to other people for their emotional and physical benefit. This requires medicine people to hold sacred space with the confidence born of the grizzly spirit, being unafraid of what tumultuous emotions may arise in a patient during a healing ceremony. For trauma victims, the bear can afford necessary strength to surmount a severe crisis and move forward.

Many Native Americans also believe that the hair of a deceased grizzly bear should be gathered because it carries healing attributes. It can impart a strength and endurance that herbs and extractions cannot match. With that in mind, and having easy access to grizzly country in Wyoming, I began collecting the hair of living bears (from fence lines and from their recently vacated dens), using it with patients to promote powerful healing. I've noted how children are particularly impressed with the mysterious and awesome power of Grizz. They are entranced by stories of helpful grizzlies that, when solidly implanted in their minds, can create expectations of positive change. From the first moment a child holds the hair of a living grizzly in their hands (being the very first human to touch the hair, as I gathered it only wearing gloves), change begins to occur. If supportive rituals of transformation are simultaneously enacted, dramatic psychological healing occurs, often swiftly.

For persons who have suffered a soul loss or soul theft by an emotional vampire, especially when it involves an interpersonal betrayal, the grizzly can become a spirit helper offering courage, sustenance, and perseverance.

Power and Boundaries

Native people universally regard grizzlies as extraordinarily intelligent beings, keen observers of all forces in Nature with a range of emotions wider than our own. Bears quietly manage their emotions, with the exception of the rare vociferous outburst reserved for insensitive creatures that invade their home boundaries or threaten their young ones. Just as Grizz appreciates respectful predictability in people, so do the victims of trauma who are easily threatened by uncertainty. Good boundaries, dependability, modulation of emotions, fearlessness, loyalty to vulnerable loved ones, periodic "hibernation" followed by socialization: these are all bear strategies that can be adapted by trauma survivors. So it is that the grizzly can become a role model for individuals in search of their lost self, in search of a soul retrieval.

What sets Grizz apart from humans—who also hold immense power—is that Grizz tends to be quite measured in the use of his power. From my privileged time with him, Grizz has become a trusted forest companion and spirit guide. In his company in the remote country of Wyoming, I can find solace from the stresses of my everyday life, particularly the strain that comes from being in the competitive company of professional colleagues. For the most part, my patients are remarkably inspiring, even those violent persons who are willing to confront their demons. But give me Grizz energy any day.

When rejuvenation is required, Nature beckons. Hiking in bear country, I recover a lost rhythm and find myself centered in this place the pioneers once called the "wilderness." For example, in the mountains of northern British Columbia near Prince Rupert, there is a grizzly-bear preserve. It has been a home for bears for longer than we know. As they travel seasonally from their high points of hibernation to the sedge-grass fields in the deep valleys below, grizzlies follow the exact same paths they have walked for hundreds of years, if not longer. Their footprints are deeply imprinted in the mountainside, and with each annual trek they place their feet in the exact same tracks of their ancestors. It must be like a comforting trance walk. And for those of us who have trekked that path, putting one foot into the next bear print ahead and so forth, we become Bear and fall into a deeply relaxed state. Grizz offers us a walking meditation if we follow his Healing Path, literally and metaphorically.

The Psychedelic Revival

While the Native American way of expanding consciousness frequently solicits an animal-spirit guide such as Grizzly, mainstream American culture has typically been more preoccupied with *altering* consciousness through the use of psychedelics. The great deal of drug exploration that occurred in the 1960s and 1970s was often characterized by its excesses. The flamboyant personalities of some early psychedelic proponents—Dr. Timothy Leary is one well-known example—with their hedonistic and narcissistic antics understandably alienated many people. Much of the drug use in that era was not designed to produce psychological healing or spiritual development. Too often it was about escape, intense mind-altering recreational experiences, pleasure seeking, or flipping off oppressive parents, institutions, and the government.

More than fifty years later, we are taking another look at many of the mind-altering plants, substances, and

THE PSYCHEDELIC REVIVAL | 161

pharmaceuticals that include natural entheogens, empathogens, and hallucinogens. Renewed credibility is being given to iboga (ibogaine), ayahuasca (vine of the gods), psilocybin (magic mushrooms), and mescaline (peyote and San Pedro cactus). Also regaining credibility are other lesser-known natural sources such as the molecule DMT acquired from the skin of the Sonoran Desert toad (some theorize it may also be endogenously produced within the pineal gland of the human brain). Used by many cultures for ritual purposes, DMT is an extremely potent psychedelic, leading psychiatrist Rick Strassman to call it the "spirit molecule."[1]

The revived interest in therapeutic substances took a huge leap forward with the 2018 publication of Michael Pollan's *New York Times* bestseller, *How to Change Your Mind*. Long known for his health-conscious books, Pollan stepped into new landscape to help us look at some of these medicines with greater objectivity while describing his own entrancing personal experiences.

Collectively, many of these medicines—both natural and manmade—can produce frightening and rugged rides en route to psychological healing and spiritual transcendence. With their sacramental use, sacred intentions (the set), and within a safe and well-designed context (the setting), however, the medicines frequently offer long-term results that can be deeply healing and, at the same time, mystical. They are currently being used with PTSD patients, the severely depressed, and persons suffering from many types of addictions, particularly to opioids.

Entheogens can open people up for internal spiritual navigation and growth, helping them discover divine connections from within—what some would call *enlightenment. Theoneurology,* a term coined by Strassman, bridges spirituality and science in proposing that the Divine communicates with us using the brain.

It posits that the brain can generate unity experiences, often after a catalytic thrust from plant medicines such as psilocybin, iboga, peyote, or ayahuasca, as well as DMT. Many neuropsychiatrists, along with ordinary citizen navigators of the numinous, assert that pharmaceutically produced LSD can do the same, perhaps while providing meaning to traumatic experiences.

Indigenous healers have known from firsthand involvement how plant entheogens diminish interspecies separations with a harmonizing influence, thereby diminishing psychological suffering. Entheogens can reveal many of the obscure or hidden parts of life. Paradoxically, the mystery in which plant medicines are enshrouded opens people to new possibilities, new ways of seeing, the noetic, and eventual clarity about many previously esoteric questions.

MDMA

Empathogens are heart-opening medicines that engender empathy, compassion, unity, and emotional healing following ravaging relationship ordeals. In that way we can regard empathogens as relational medicines that reflect the cosmologies of indigenous peoples—their way of walking, being with, and remaining connected to all parts of this living world. The amphetamine MDMA (not to be confused with the illicit and dangerous street drug called *Ecstasy*), when ingested in pure clinical-grade form, provides a safe and gentle path to restoring interpersonal conflicts, a way out of the trauma and resultant fear born of interpersonal betrayals. It works via a distinctively different set of pathways in the brain from the way classical psychedelics such as LSD function. MDMA is notorious for its ability to help interpersonally injured people drop their defenses, sort out relationship confusion, forgive, and rejoin the world with greater insights and internal peace. It intensifies, or amplifies, human perceptions without taking people to illusory or terrifying places. Empathogens seem to reanimate the world, unifying people with one another and the natural world around them—or, as the Lakota would say, *mitakuye oyasin*, meaning "all my relatives." The result of this ego-diminishing experience is referred to as "unitive" or "non-dual" consciousness.

This modern synthetic medicine, MDMA, like ancient plant medicines, helps spiritual seekers connect to the Greater Mind, a larger umbrella consciousness. As one facet of consciousness, the human brain is regarded by ancients and moderns as something resembling a transducer. Modern cultures might understand it by using television as a metaphor. The device in our living rooms can pick up invisible signals and translate them into sounds and pictures that we can see and understand. Television takes one form of information from a distant source to persons at another location, reducing larger ideas and connections so that the comparatively puny human brain can discern them. The result is a feeling of being connected to something larger than ourselves.

Again and again, I have heard reports of how entheogens and empathogens create a similar sense of spiritual enlightenment. Seen in the grand scheme of things, earthly problems, such as trauma and addiction, seem less ominous and potentially more surmountable. A distancing phenomenon occurs; standing back a bit, problems can be seen more clearly. Binary thinking in terms of good guys and bad guys, perpetrators and victims, seems to fall away. Divisions dissolve. Commonalities are seen. Adversaries are often regarded as shadow parts of oneself. The result is unity consciousness and healing.

The Neuroscience of MDMA

In 2012, fascinating brain-scanning research got underway at Imperial College in London. That work, when combined with other neuroscientific theorizing, is beginning to lift the hood on the human brain, revealing what MDMA actually does to provide a dispassionate reexamination of trauma.

Neurobiochemical mechanisms take place during MDMA treatment that produce the closely related hormones oxytocin and prolactin, the cuddling or bonding chemicals traditionally released during breast-feeding or after sex. These chemicals seem to counteract fear, distrust, and separation anxiety, emotions that trauma commonly produces. And relationship connection (emplacement) is an antidote to rage, invalidation, and the feeling of being unrooted.

Meanwhile, the amphetamine component in clinical-grade MDMA stimulates the prefrontal cortex so that it stays operative and can—maybe for the first time following trauma—introduce some logic and allow some integration of painful memories. Additionally, a large surge of the neurotransmitter serotonin lifts the mood of patients while they review previously dark and despairing memories.

Preliminary research suggests that MDMA also produces an increase in dopamine, a neurotransmitter that creates pleasure in the moment while anticipating a pleasurable future. So, while patients are grappling with their memories of highly fractious relationships or other kinds of trauma, rather than the panic such memories would traditionally bring about they feel calm, surprisingly content, and somewhat optimistic. They lose much of the helplessness that consumed them before ingestion. In a way, the synergistic ingredients of MDMA "trick" the brain into processing information differently—and, in fact, more accurately.

In essence, MDMA seems to deactivate primitive regions of the brain, such as the amygdala, which is the seat of fear and rage or, as some say, the five Fs: fight, flight, freeze, faint, and feed. It also appears to quiet the entire deep limbic system, including the basal ganglia, which is the region notorious for generating anxiety and forward thinking in such forms as worry and apprehension. As a result, the prefrontal cortex can, in turn, do its job of making sense of what happened, answering some of the proverbial questions such as "why me?" Overall, MDMA diminishes emotional overload while ramping up rationality and discernment.

Studies have indicated that the interaction of upper and lower brain regions, rather than left and right hemispheres, are implicated in reactions to trauma. When the deep limbic system is lit up with fear, anxiety, or profound sadness, something akin to a circuit-breaker effect takes place. The primitive lower regions of the brain "blow a fuse" that slows down the higher-functioning prefrontal lobe. The process of the prefrontal lobe shutting down could be compared to losing internet service. The wisest and most discerning part of the brain goes offline, which allows the emotional coloring of the lower brain to rule.

Often people with PTSD experience overactivity in the anterior cingulate region of the brain, which causes people to perseverate and obsess about their painful memories, looping a static mental narrative of hurt, harm, and self-blame—a sad and disempowering story that is told and retold incessantly. When the anterior cingulate is less active, a person can shift gears and move on, no longer remaining stuck in the "mental mud" of the past. MDMA quiets this region of the brain, allowing the trauma victim to compose a new and healing narrative.

The result of such brain changes is commonly reflected in the vocalizations that occur during the late stages of an MDMA session. Moments of mental clarity are put into cogent sentences. What is often heard are excited exclamations that may sound like, "Where did that come from?!" What psychotherapists often overhear is the patient's own brilliant interpretations of their trauma. They start gently and compassionately to counsel themselves. The wisdom espoused can be stunning for everyone. It is an empowering time for victims upon realizing that an inner healer resides within them; they hold the keys to a new way of being. Not always must they go in search of a healer, guru, pastor, or psychotherapist—someone external to themselves—hoping to have their world explained to them. A deep, inner wisdom percolates up, like previously unseen air bubbles in a pond that suddenly reach the surface awareness and pop open with an "I see it now!" lucidity.

What About Safety?

Curiously, almost all these medicines are nonaddictive. In fact, some work to cure addictions, such as the Malaysian tree leaf, kratom; the Amazonia hallucinogenic, ayahuasca; and the root from a West African bush called iboga. And the fears of madness and death promulgated by the media and our government decades ago—particularly with regard to LSD and psilocybin—have long since been debunked, as have tales of psychosis and of people jumping off buildings as a result of ingesting MDMA. Any actual problems likely arose from the ingestion of contaminated street lookalikes, Molly and Ecstasy, which all too often were laced with menacing and even deadly fillers such as the elephant tranquilizer, fentanyl.

In truth, most of these rediscovered medicines can provoke more fear than they are physiologically dangerous. It turns out that in the 1960s and '70s spiritual seekers such as Ram Dass and Terence McKenna knew much more about these medicines than uninformed and influential critics such as Art Linkletter and Nancy ("Just say no") Reagan. Contemporary conversation has shifted to the value of such medicines in diminishing the confusion of ego—self-generated mind chatter—while helping people recover from significant, mental health distress.

The historical use of plant medicines, and even the medicinal use of toad secretions, goes back thousands of years. It is common to see mushrooms and toads (*Bufo marinus*) depicted in Maya art. Both were thought to be integral parts of sacred ceremonial activity that enabled shamans to transcend the limitations of everyday thinking.

When some of the rediscovered old medicines are combined with indigenous ceremonies, they can create a powerful potentiating effect. The accompanying reset of the mind achieved in six hours provides a significant contrast to what is accomplished over six years of psychotherapy. Ancient and modern medicines, offered in tandem, may represent the future of psychiatric medicine. Perhaps as importantly, when compared to existing psychotropic pharmaceuticals, they routinely provide more effective and safer, as well as less expensive and nonaddictive, healing alternatives.

Belief, Suggestion, and the Placebo Effect

Indigenous healers have long known of the importance of engendering possibilities in the human mind when readying persons for life transitions. They have taught us how sacred activities surrounding the use of plant medicines can create altered states that prepare the mind for imminent change. And altered states can lower defenses and open the mind to mysterious prospects.

Ceremonies provide a consecrated setting—a big spiritual and psychological event—that reminds participants of traditional, time-tested, and enduring practices while combining them with community support. Ceremonies, with their attendant mystery, ready the mind for something out of the ordinary. With all their pomp and pageantry, they do much of the "heavy lifting" that promotes an eventual transformation. Ritual activities implanted in ceremonies provide additional buildup for a shift that can transport all participants to new mental terrain. Rituals can be regarded as the ingredients in the ceremonial recipe for change.

Traditional healers are masters in manipulating the mind, preparing it for a significant alteration before any medicine is presented. For example, when a Navajo or Hopi medicine person looks to Father Sky and speaks of boundless possibilities, a world with no perceived limits, he opens us up to new prospects. We are made aware of a much bigger mind that orchestrates the harmony and balance of the universes. The healer and the patient humble themselves in the presence of such powerful forces and look to the Great Mystery, which is the Ojibwa conceptualization of God, for solutions beyond one's immediate grasp.

Ancestral powers—an array of honored allies and spirit forces that includes all sentient beings, not just humans—are welcomed into indigenous healing circles. Ceremonial supplicants humbly join ranks with forces beyond everyday understandings and comprehension, trusting that something previously thought to be impossible just might occur. While inviting in the ancestors, indigenous healers avoid imploring, pleading, or begging language. That would be considered a low-energy mind-set associated with desperation and would not promote healing. A lighter spirit, or ascendant energy, creates a gentler vibration to summon assistance and suggests trust in the restorative capacities of a benevolent cosmos, the well-ordered Whole.

To further set the stage for change, a thanksgiving prayer is offered in advance of the ritualized treatment, strongly suggesting a satisfying outcome is just around the corner. When hope is in place, healing is never far behind. Upon the completion of ceremony, another prayer of thanks is offered, providing two positive bookends to concretize the good outcome.

Often Native American healers will tell stories of previous healings they have witnessed. These uplifting stories can be used to raise a person's spirit, put the individual at ease, and allow the inner healer to relax them into a new state of being. With stress and despair ameliorated, the body and mind are inclined to move away from the previous stuck spot called "illness." The doctor within is being activated.

When a healer presents as authoritative, perhaps simply by putting on their shamanic regalia and entering with a confident demeanor, optimistic notions are implanted; they take root and foster the belief that "I've found the right person for my recovery." When other tribal members, including previous patients, share their stories of success working with the chosen shaman, confidence in the outcome is ramped up even further.

Another factor that distinguishes indigenous healing traditions from Western healing is the strong belief in working within a community of supporters. Never left to feel alone or separated from others, the suffering individual experiences comfort and the bolstered confidence of being part of a group event. One-on-one, time-limited approaches simply don't make sense to indigenous people. People must plan on "staying the course" until physical and mental restoration is achieved. And better still, take the healing outdoors where everyone can feel their connection to the larger Whole, feeling sustained by the creative and benevolent forces of Nature. Healing rarely occurs when a person is disconnected from Source, from Creator.

Critics of these methods often reduce the complexity of indigenous healing principles to sleight of hand or magic. Yes, it is magic of a sort, but a *sacred magic*, a form of seemingly miraculous change rooted in the *super natural*. The ingredients for healing are on the planet; we are required only to step on Mother Earth and combine energies with other sentient life relatives while sacralizing the process. The mundane rarely heals. Nor does the mechanical. Nor a simple capsule of MDMA or similar medicine. A complex amalgam of strategies, many of which simply create an expectant mind-set, are magical in the best sense of the word.

Indigenous-Inspired MDMA Psychotherapy

A small number of underground psychotherapists offer MDMA-assisted healing. While the effectiveness of MDMA alone is profound, notably in addressing trauma, addictions, and treatment-resistant depression, licensing boards generally regard its current use as unethical. Although it remains an unapproved approach, it offers patients a nonhallucinatory, safe, and effective way to resolve long-standing mental-health problems. Research—especially the Multidisciplinary Association for Psychedelic Studies (MAPS) Phase II studies—revealed that, following the use of MDMA and accompanied by psychotherapy, 68 percent of PTSD sufferers no longer met the diagnostic criteria after three, five-hour treatments. Symptoms fell away and remained quiescent for a period of at least twelve months. Currently, Phase III research is providing even more optimistic, albeit tentative, findings.

To see it is to believe it. Trauma therapists who witness the use of MDMA frequently become evangelists for this method of healing. This occurs, in part, because the observable results break open the therapists' previous, university-indoctrinated mind regarding just how much progress victims of PTSD and Complex PTSD (CPTSD) can realize. Hope abounds, both among patients and healers. And when each person shares confidence in this procedure, a combined potentiating effect, or bolstered enthusiasm, occurs, giving the medicine even more power to reset the brain.

When, moreover, this empathogen is embedded in a sacred ceremony with its inherent impetus and energy, a mind shift can occur that is so dramatic that, at first glance, it can appear artificial, transient, or illusory. Regular ceremonial work with this medicine—when set and setting are carefully arranged by an experienced ritualist—generates therapeutic outcomes that far surpass even some of the more recently appealing approaches, including eye movement desensitization and reprocessing (EMDR), trauma-sensitive yoga, tapping, vagus-nerve stimulation, and other body-therapy interventions. Blending modern medicines with ancient rituals amplifies power. The resulting brain reset often lasts indefinitely, due, in part, to the depth of personal integration work that accompanies MDMA-assisted psychotherapy.

One patient I observed being treated described her personal work to me in this way:

> I understand that trauma is a powerfully impactful life event that can leave people feeling profoundly damaged and changed. Now I am beginning to question whether trauma can also be a positive, life-altering event that leaves people feeling profoundly changed for the better, even enlightened. I also wonder if this approach [indigenously influenced, MDMA-assisted psychotherapy] could be regarded as a "healing trauma," one that sort of paves over the previous painful events? My therapy was every bit as memorable as my trauma, but it feels like this shift is positive and lasting.[2]

The Future of Psychotherapy

The late Terence McKenna, a pioneer in the study of entheogens and psychedelics for healing and transcendent purposes, always had an eye (or three) to the future. I am reminded of one of his many illuminating comments: "If you don't have a plan, you become part of somebody else's plan." That said, and following the decades-long drug hysteria in the United States—much of which was never justified—there must now be a discriminating reexamination of previously unfamiliar or feared medicines. As discussed, MDMA is one of those medicines that promise relief for many mental health patients in the immediate future. Another is ketamine.

Ketamine, an anesthesia that has been used by physicians and veterinarians, is now being employed as a legal, off-label antidepressant. It has rapidly become the "go to" choice of progressive psychologists and psychiatrists when a serious depression, often with suicidal ideation, is present. Given by infusion, nasal sprays, or by snorting a ground compound, ketamine brings about results that routinely exceed the most dramatic results seen with traditional antidepressants, even when those antidepressants are matched with psychotherapy. And for decades, psychologists such as the late Ralph Metzner have thoughtfully and meticulously blended ketamine and MDMA, achieving results that patients often described as "mystical" or "enlightenment" experiences. Not only did they recover from severe psychological problems, but the majority appeared to transcend their previous best moments in life by entering into an even more satisfying, meaningful, and stabilizing emotional existence. In that sense, much like plant entheogens, even a select few pharmaceuticals can offer noetic or revelatory effects.

Mushrooms, in the form of pharmaceutical-grade psilocybin, may not be FDA approved until 2025 or later. Other similar entheogens have been criminalized (yes, even plants), being relegated to the categorical status of opioids, cocaine, and other dangerously addictive and potentially fatal drugs. What Nature has created is sometimes regarded by our government as dangerous and illegal, posing the ludicrous question, "How do we lock up forests?"

Until common-sense regulatory measures are in place, and a massive, public-health campaign educates Americans about the safety and efficacy of many plant entheogens and empathogens, many time-tested indigenous medicines such as iboga, ayahuasca, mushrooms, and cactus may be accessible only to the wealthy who can travel abroad. That is why the anticipated FDA approval of MDMA around 2021, or soon thereafter, beckons us to begin preparing protocols now, including indigenous-inspired ceremonies and rituals, carefully assembled in ways that do not insensitively appropriate sacred practices.

With decades of work in prison settings, especially with violent men, I now see it as quite evident that unresolved trauma and brain dysfunctions (often due to injuries from childhood abuse), compounded by chemical and sexual addictions, are being treated at the most superficial levels. Twelve-step meetings and group psychotherapy, more often than not, fail to ameliorate the underlying bio-neuro-psychological issues propelling criminal behavior. I can only imagine the day when untreated trauma and addictions are being effectively addressed *before* prisoners are paroled back into community life. Until their brains are reset in ways that ayahuasca, psilocybin, iboga, MDMA, and other ancient and modern medicines can do, we will continue to recycle errant citizens from communities to prisons and back again without their criminal patterns being interrupted.

In readiness for FDA approval of some of these medicines, I am planting seeds now to suggest replacing our current and dangerous antianxiety, antipsychotic, and antidepressant prescriptions—that do little more than mask and suppress symptoms—with elements of Nature's pharmacopeia. This vision will entail a huge paradigm shift, one that must be sparked now so that we will be ready to implement powerfully effective approaches once FDA approval of psychedelics, empathogens, and entheogens occurs. Blended with ancient wisdom and applied in sacred healing ceremonies with complementary rituals, such indigenous medicines can bring about authentic and lasting healing. Cowboys, grab the reins; this, too, will be a wild ride!

"Depression," as the renowned existential psychologist Rollo May said, "is the inability to construct a future."[3] So, let's get on with construction. What a hopeful time we live in, innovatively looking ahead while our feet remain grounded in ancient healings ways that have stood the test of time, some of them for tens of thousands of years. Methods that have endured that long and have repeatedly been shown to be effective can be referred to as *evidence based*. When considering today's MAPS research results about the efficacy of MDMA treatments, another term comes to mind: *best practice*. Ah, the best is yet to come!

12

Traditional African Plant Medicines to Combat the Heroin Epidemic

The United States is currently going through a love-hate relationship with opioids. Very potent, pain-relieving drugs, they have been widely, and often carelessly, prescribed by physicians for years. While they can be incredibly effective and provide some euphoria, opioids can become dangerously alluring and—for a large minority of individuals—lay the groundwork for a life-ravaging addiction. Some of the popular prescription drugs being abused include Nucynta, Fentanyl, Percocet, Percodan, Oxycodone, Oxycontin, and hydrocodones (Vicodin and Narco). Among the approximately five million Americans using these opioids, between 7 and 10 percent will develop an addiction. And when a person becomes physically dependent, a frantic chase ensues that can dead end (literally) at heroin.

No life experience can compare to heroin; its euphoria is far, far greater than anything known or imagined, and its withdrawal is a living hell. Oddly, to "treat" opioid addiction, physicians now prescribe similar addictive drugs, such as methadone and Suboxone (buprenorphine). The withdrawal from these drugs can be as harrowing and painful as the withdrawal from heroin addiction. They may buy some time while we await more humane and effective strategies. The current epidemic cries out for sane, sensible, and innovative solutions that don't entail addiction hopping.

While I have not suffered from the scourge of addiction, my interest in medical anthropology has introduced me to plant medicines that can guide individuals into a sometimes frightening self-analysis followed by a whole new perspective on life filled with peace, as if a reset button has been discovered. The medicine derived from the West African rainforest shrub iboga can do just that. Sound magical? For many heroin addicts, it is—an almost sacred magic.

Only rarely have I recommended a medicine to patients that I have not personally probed myself. The result has been a personal and professional avoidance of nearly all antidepressant, antipsychotic, and antianxiety drugs. I have, on the other hand, explored iboga and can confidently encourage its use with many addictions, as long as it is always under the supervision of professionals in a safe, and, hopefully, sacred setting. An African shaman first introduced me to iboga with its ability to reset one's life onto a more peaceful trajectory. It may have played a role in dramatically altering my professional practice, moving me away from a competitive, ego-steered financial enterprise to a more service-driven and reverent healing approach.

When I learned of iboga's pharmaceutical derivative, ibogaine, I sought out a heroin addiction treatment center in Canada that clinically offered this psychointegrator as an alternative to addictive remedies. Their results have compelled me to write about this new, yet old, approach to addiction and trauma treatment. What follows is a realistic and optimistic exploration of this West African plant medicine.

The human body makes its own natural pain killers, including endogenous opioids and endocannabinoids. No wonder we are drawn to their relatives. Since the discovery of mood-altering exogenous opioids—including cocaine and heroin—we have long lamented how they generate massive cravings and excruciating withdrawal symptoms that seem virtually intractable. Moreover, the more exogenous opioids are used, the less the body is able to produce its own pain killers.

In recent years, pharmaceutical companies have encouraged health-care professionals to prescribe addictive drugs to eliminate addiction to drugs! I am confident that shamans everywhere would look at this development as backward and nonsensical. Sometimes in capitalistic societies, sacred solutions don't prove to be profitable. So, from the perspective of traditional medicine, we are all being invited to look beyond Big Pharma for better solutions. Upon doing so, it shouldn't surprise us that Mother Earth has an earthly solution for most every earthly problem. She is quite wise that way. Her solution to many unproductive life difficulties, especially addiction and trauma, is to offer the African plant medicine, iboga. This root, and its derivative, ibogaine, have shown a remarkable ability to stop addiction in its tracks. For that reason, it is often referred to as an *addiction-interrupter* medicine.

Traditional African life revolves around ceremonies and their supporting rituals to address physical and emotional maladies. Among the people of West Central Africa, a *bwiti* is understood to be a person who ingests iboga in an effort to make personal discoveries about himself, life, Nature, and the interactions of all life forces. It is also a friend who can guide a person out of personal crisis. In Gabon and Cameroon, traditional biwiti initiation rituals are used to point people's lives in a new and more satisfying direction. With a sacred mind-set, and within a safe setting, traditional medicine people use rituals, chants, whistling, music, dance, and iboga to change the consciousness of a person and lift them into a transcendent place of unity. By doing this in a carefully orchestrated way, long-held resentments and adversarial feelings can be dissolved, almost as if a reset button has been tapped in the person's brain.

Psychedelics and Psychointegrators

Iboga and ibogaine are not to be regarded as a romanticized, or, for that matter, dangerous psychedelic that creates an enjoyable high while providing an escape from life's travails. This plant medicine does not do that. Iboga is not a recreational drug. It is better understood as an entheogen or a psychointegrator that can awaken and amplify an internal wisdom and foster a very personal mystical experience that heals. Different from hallucinogens and without some of the exotic carnival urgency that can surround them, iboga can help people see and explore the personal artifacts of their life that have kept them stuck, impeding their growth and luring them into addiction solutions. The plant can foster a mental cleaning that facilitates the restarting of a new and more spiritually authentic life.

Under its guidance, a person may move in and out of different realms or realities; but, in its embrace, iboga can expose the very real consequences of one's errant ways. Instead of helping you escape your life, it confronts you with it. And it allows room for an entirely new journey to unfold. Ingesting iboga is like fast-tracking AA's fourth step in which you are advised to take a searching and fearless moral inventory of yourself. It is as if iboga has a built-in bullshit detector, whereby you must see and examine harsh truths.

Twelve-step programs often use the familiar Serenity Prayer: "God, grant me the serenity to accept the things I cannot change, the courage to change the things I can, and the wisdom to know the difference." America's new Serenity Prayer has become, "God, grant me a magic-bullet pill to take away my addiction to magic-bullet solutions." Iboga has that kind of magic-bullet allure that can pull people into recovery, but, at the same time, it actually keeps its promise. Some people who have worked with it say that it is like years of psychotherapy crammed into a few hours. It gives you a second chance.

A "Trip" Inward

In essence, iboga gifts people with its plant consciousness, which, in turn, expands their own consciousness. The medicine directs the bwiti inward to a place where he can listen to his own inner guide, quite unlike a chemical-dependency counselor who implores addicts to follow a one-size-fits-all approach to recovery. The spirit of the plant seems to connect people to their own essential spirit, what some might call their *soul*. From there, individualized insights and teachings arise. This occurs without human intervention or interpretation as the person rests in quiet introspection. There is no attending psychotherapist offering generic advice; there is just comfort. Each individual, while under the guidance of the plant medicine, is left to figure things out within this treatment medium.

In the West African tribal culture of Gabon, the sacred use of iboga, especially after adherents have been washed with herbs in a river, has been called a "spiritual shower." It has also been described as a feeling of being purified and reborn, reunified or aligned with the entire world. For a person with years of trauma and drug or alcohol addiction behind them, arriving at such a state changes their basic conceptualization of life. It does so with such a rapidity and a dramatic urgency that old ways are no longer appealing and suddenly their life feels transformed, their mind reset. The medicine uncovers a new personal energy that is a natural part of the participant. Consequently, there is greater chance of a "buy in" and less resistance to prior external solutions that have been forcefully imposed by family, psychotherapists, physicians, or probation officers. A lightness of spirit emerges from within that points out previously unseen and unimagined aspects of participants that will eventually benefit them and their world. The spirit or soul of the universe is generously showered over them.

Coming out of the exhausting experience of an iboga healing, many individuals note that their minds seem to have been deprogrammed, and then reprogrammed, in a healthier and more positive way. For those persons suffering from cocaine and heroin addictions, the deprogramming and resultant transformation snaps them out of their monotonous drug trance and reconnects them to uplifting life forces. There is an apparent movement away from old selfish ways and limiting beliefs into a gentle coherence with the more universal laws of reciprocity and coexistence.

Still others report their state of mind as that of being a child again, unburdened by prior mental confusion and expectations.

It is as if they are receiving sanctified messages that stand in sharp contrast with the corrupted thinking they experienced in the world of addiction. A clarity arrives, and the differences among personal truths, personal lies, and supreme truths is less clouded. Often many note a reprieve from their previously incessant self-loathing—which is generally a major impediment to drug and alcohol addiction recovery—with the ensuing void being replaced by a sense of awe and of opening to the child-like innocence and wonder of life. At that point, a spiritual wasteland has been crossed, and a resacralization of the self occurs.

Issues of Legality and Proper Protocol

Because of societal and political fears of psychoactive substances, iboga and ibogaine are not well understood. Consequently, in many countries, the United States included, this plant medicine and its derivative are illegal. In a few countries, including Costa Rica, Mexico, Holland, England, and Canada, some progressive healers have established in-patient treatment facilities. Unfortunately, though, instead of seeking these facilities, many heroin addicts in their desperation will settle for a flood dose of iboga in a hotel room with little or no medically supervised care.

Nevertheless, progressive health-care providers are moving toward sophisticated programs that will serve a greater number of people, some of which offer supportive rituals to complement medical care. These programs are providing what appears to be a revolutionary new way of treating addiction without using more addictive-replacement drugs such as Suboxone. They are also moving far beyond foundational but incomplete twelve-step methods that are limited to psychological and spiritual guidelines. Iboga, especially in the form of ibogaine, establishes a blocking mechanism at the opioid receptors of the brain.

I visited a treatment facility near Vancouver, British Columbia, called Liberty Root. It offers an approximately eight-day treatment regimen that weans patients off heroin or cocaine. The program is directed and monitored by staff members who are recognized within Canada's ibogaine treatment network. Liberty Root has nurses on hand, particularly at pivotal points in the treatment process, and a world-renowned psychiatrist is on standby for additional care. Once heroin has been significantly removed from the body (often with the careful administration of morphine, the level of which is systematically reduced and eventually eliminated), small doses of ibogaine are introduced in capsule form, which has a mild stimulating effect. After about three days of observation, hydrating, flushing with water, and the introduction of healthy foods, a flood dose of ibogaine is administered.

Not uncommonly, within thirty to forty-five minutes, cravings have disappeared. Hours later, withdrawal symptoms cease. The patient is placed in a darkened room with a staff member stationed nearby to offer reassurance and comfort as needed. A visionary experience commences. Many of the visions that arise can be very unsettling, even frightening. Eventually, perhaps as many as twelve hours pass with nausea and dizziness being common. Exhausted and relieved after these "night travels," the patient falls asleep. Upon awakening many hours later, all craving for heroin and many other addictive drugs has disappeared. It feels like Liberation Day.

A New Beginning

Emptied of the spirit of addiction and even the nightmares of trauma, the person now has room for the inner light to shine, which is concomitant with an awakening of additional healing abilities that have been suppressed by drugs. Tears flow, but not tears of sadness; they are tears of relief and joy. They are cleansing tears that come with the recognition of the gift that just been bestowed at long last, the beginning of a realistic opportunity for freedom from addiction. The ibogaine journey is much like a successful soul retrieval. After a day or two of being reoriented to this healthier way, the patient is discharged, usually without any medications whatsoever. However, for peace and sobriety to continue, well-trained and ongoing, indigenously inspired psychotherapy must await them. Aftercare must be well planned and rigorously applied.

Can recovery be this quick and simple? For the most part, the answer is yes. Three quarters of Liberty Roots patients have reported continued sobriety months after treatment, and I suspect recovery could be additionally effective if conducted within a ritualized setting, perhaps borrowing some features similar to African traditions.

Importantly, though, it must be said that ibogaine is not foolproof. Relapses do occur, despite all of the plant medicine's natural gifts. Even when patients have lost their craving for opioids, they can still have a psychological dependence and old acquaintances who can lure them back into their former using pattern.

Kratom

Iboga isn't the only plant medicine offering assistance out of the extraordinary grip of opioid addiction. Kratom (*Mitragyna speciosa*), an ancient Indonesian plant medicine, has been used by shamans for hundreds of years, if not much longer. It originates from the leaf of a tree that is from the coffee family. While this natural opioid has analgesic and anti-inflammatory benefits, it can also lift mood. Does this sound like just another addictive drug? Not necessarily.

While kratom, if used heavily and over extended periods, can result in addiction, it is really mild compared to opioid addictions caused by prescription pain relievers, illicit drugs such as heroin, and the even more addictive synthetic opioids used to treat opioid addiction such as methadone and Suboxone. Kratom addiction can occur when used excessively, but symptoms are much less severe, and recovery doesn't last as long and is much easier to treat. What is particularly interesting and quite paradoxical about this complicated natural medicine is that kratom has been used, particularly in Southeast Asian countries, to assist people in withdrawing from other opioids. Yes—a natural opioid used to treat other opioid addictions!

In the United States, the Drug Enforcement Administration (DEA) has rushed to sound a reproachful alarm about unregulated kratom after several batches were found to be laced with the synthetic opioid fentanyl (a synthetic painkiller), which is estimated to be thirty to fifty times as powerful as heroin and is a relatively cheap potentiator. Additionally, heroin is itself routinely being laced with fentanyl, which is partially responsible for the dramatic surge in deaths from overdoses. Even worse, carfentanil, the veterinary medicine used to anesthetize very large animals such as elephants and rhinos—which is reportedly ten thousand times as potent as morphine—is being added to the heroin sold in North America.

Fortunately, the initial hysteria surrounding kratom's use has subsided in recent months, and mainstream media outlets such as CNN have cautiously championed the plant as an effective and promising aid in the treatment of opioid addictions, if it is carefully regulated to avoid contamination. Perhaps once again, Nature provides one of the best solutions.

Shamanic Dismemberment on the Road to Health

Addiction can be envisioned as a spirit-guided dismemberment experience, similar to what shamans undergo when they are disassembled and, like Humpty Dumpty, must be put back together again. The process requires the jettisoning of ineffective behaviors and unwanted features and the reassembly of a new life, including a soul retrieval. Metaphorically, one will need "all the king's horses and all the king's men" and plenty of dress rehearsals to reintegrate oneself into a vastly altered social environment. With this process, there may be potential healing gifts to be shared, in much the same way as what AA adherents refer to as the "twelfth step," in which they experience a spiritual awakening and are encouraged to carry their healing gifts to others. Falling apart, in true shamanic tradition, can become a prelude to full health and full integration of previous life experiences, at first traumatic and then comforting.

Traditional shamans and their ancient healing ways can still guide us as we address contemporary health problems through the lens of their best wisdom born of experience. Some of the medical and psychological discoveries and rediscoveries being made today are, in fact, reincarnations of ancient spiritual knowledge, and iboga restoration rituals are one example. When we live attuned to and in harmony with Mother Earth's voice, when we are aligned with her spirit and are careful not to wander far from her bosom, *super natural* healing can occur.

Growing Beyond Self
in Zimbabwe and Guatemala

The two antipodal locations of Africa and Central America hold complementary views of consciousness. In Zimbabwe, the "I Am" of Mandaza Kandemwa refers to the underlying unity of all people and all cultures that moves away from limiting tribal identities. In Guatemala, Mandaza's ideas are amplified by the Mayan cosmovision that reflects our relationship with relatives from ancient times, a conceptualization of interconnectedness that supersedes both time and location.

Consciousness in the Shona Healing Tradition

Mandaza is a Zimbabwean water-spirits healer (*nganga*) of the Shona tribal tradition. As such, his function is to serve others, to live a life of prayerful meditation for all creatures of consciousness—which is broadly defined, including humans, other animals, plants, water, mountains, the air, and so on.

Mandaza is in regular communication with a community of spirits called *midzimu*, what are often referred to as ancestors. These spirits are not limited to bloodline or even to the human species.

FIGURE 9. Baba Mandaza Making *Muti*. He receives instructions for these medicines from his community of spirits called *midzimu*. (Author's photograph)

Midzimu give Mandaza and other traditional healers vital information about the patients they treat. They acquaint him with the illnesses and the medicines (*muti*) that can foster healing. Mandaza easily flows in and out of trance possession, both feet anchored solidly in the realities he traverses. It is a volitional talent that allows him to access many ways of knowing a person and their ailments. Being trance possessed is an alteration of consciousness, a sensory shift that allows for a shared identity with another spirit. We are not limited to the classic five senses. Many of our interspecies sensory abilities have atrophied over humanity's "civilizing advancements" due to a lack of use.

Morning "I Am" Meditation

During one of my journeys to see Mandaza, I am with him at a poignant time as he readies himself for a trip to neighboring Botswana. There, two weeks after our visit, he will speak to a large audience along with His Holiness the Dalai Lama, discussing the subjects of peace, unity, and compassion.

It is early on a late July morning—winter in Zimbabwe—and Mandaza and I have started our day in meditation. Much to the delight of some observing teenagers, we two old men begin dancing on the grass to Zimbabwe music. As an old Zimbabwean adage goes, "If you can walk, you can dance."

On this day, Mandaza is compelled to share a time of enlightenment that he experienced while sitting alone in a German forest several years ago. It was in that setting that he composed his *I Am* treatise. It speaks of his overarching philosophy that, at its core, emphasizes a divine unity that energizes and supports all forms of life.

The *I Am,* as best I can describe it, is what Mandaza refers to as the One Spirit, a unifying force that exists and moves through all things, things that at first glance appear as individual entities. As I listen to him, I can't help but hear gentle echoes of Mahatma Gandhi.

This One Spirit, or God, remains a great conundrum, Mandaza asserts. Efforts to describe an enigma of this magnitude will surely fail. The mystery is also referred to as Creator, the Energy, or the Life Force that animates the entire earth. It is ineffable. Mandaza says that if one tries to explain it by condensing the idea into our meager languages, inevitably we will lose much of its power in Shona healing circles. Mystery is one of the greatest healers of all.

As with the Dalai Lama and many proponents of Buddhism, in Mandaza's philosophy "not knowing"—meaning an openness to unfamiliar possibilities—holds a rich repository of healing power. That is, for the water-spirits healer, not knowing isn't seen as a weakness. To the contrary, it can create hopeful anticipation and open a wide door to unlimited healing possibilities.

Knowing is largely a function of the ego and consciousness. *Not knowing,* it follows, is a function of putting the ego's need to *know* aside in the service of something greater. *Dying to ego* is a practice that reminds us that none of us are elevated above others in importance but rather are an equal and integral part of the world community of creatures. Diminishing personal pride is integral to the *I Am* spiritual path. At the same time, and not in contradiction, a demonstrated authoritative confidence shown by the healer strongly suggests that he is the one who can remedy afflictions and disease, thereby beginning the restorative process. All shamans have gifts that spirit bestows on them and that move through them. An effective healer is simply a chosen conduit of the spirits. Believing in that person's divinely awarded talents promotes healings. The Shona believe in beliefs; they have faith in faith.

Along with many people from indigenous cultures, Mandaza and I share the belief that an energizing spirit of life flows through all of creation. It moves from person to person, object to object, leaving all of the earth connected and unified. Awareness of this core unity is at the foundation of Mandaza's world view. And in his company, I feel a subtle current of grace. We are one with this God Force, and, as such, we become cocreators of our own destiny. We are never apart from Creator. We are the universe in person. We are a living force containing an ongoing creative energy. The great *I Am* links us to everything and everyone, often through dreams and trance possession. All life is indivisible, or, as wise indigenous elders have long said, joined in an interconnected web. Mandaza reminds us that we are tasked, as vital constituent parts of the *I Am,* to be like spiders, connecting people and animals to one another at deeper levels. He believes that human efforts to separate people by race, creed, status, geographic boundaries, and so on create psychological and physical diseases. Coming together as part of the greater *I Am* restores the world's natural vitality.

Traditional healers, through a life committed to service, minister to the common good. As St. Francis of Assisi said, "It is in consoling others that we are consoled. It is in giving that we receive." Our concern for the well-being of others allows benevolent favor to be returned to us. We don't engage in service in the hope of an eventual reward (Mandaza serves without a fee but accepts donations); we do so because reciprocity is the natural order of things: it just feels right. This back-and-forth exchange of energy is both mood- and life-sustaining. In this world without divisions, Mandaza freely shares his *agape* love with all. It is a love that seeks nothing in return. It is the love of the divine Creator moving through him.

There are no exceptions to this tenet. All of the Creator's life forms are our brothers and sisters and deserve loving attention. *I Am* is the force of life guided by spirit through the human heart, not misdirected by the mind that, all too often, merely serves to confuse humans. As long as the mind says "I am" in the small, personal sense, being understood as the ordinary yet presumably important ego as opposed to the transpersonal *I Am*, we will be inclined to have emotional disturbances. Seen this way, it is not that "I" have a problem; rather, the concept of "I" is the fundamental problem restricting spiritual awareness.

This *I Am* awareness radiates humility. It asks that we take nothing from outside ourselves for sustenance or pleasure without first asking for permission and then offering thanks. This is reflected in the gathering of water and the harvesting of pumpkins or chickens. Ritual acts of supplication precede and follow receiving gifts from any part of Nature. With Mandaza, it may appear as the scattering of tobacco or seeds before entering his garden, or dropping to his knees with hands slightly tilted, lightly clasping his hands together in homage.

Author Robert Augustus Masters concludes his book *Spiritual Bypassing* by writing about the "soul's embrace." His words resonate well with the thoughts of Mandaza:

> Ego says: I am what I think I am.
> Soul says: I am more than I can imagine.
> Spirit says: I am.

We are [I am] Light and we [I am] Darkness
And we [I am] the flesh, be it mud or stars
Torn between the two
Yet already the One
Inseparable from the broken Many.[1]

Being Introduced to Myself by a "Stranger"

During my three visits with Mandaza over the last decade, I have witnessed him daily express his *I Am* philosophy. Being no different and certainly no better than anyone else, Mandaza greets everyone with a smile, and laughter almost always ensues, even with total strangers. They feel safe and, above all, respected by him.

On one of these visits, with Mandaza's son Israel driving the car, we set out to see the sacred ruins of the Late-Iron-Age city known as Great Zimbabwe, where kings resided on top of the hill and presided over the villages below. While en route, Mandaza told me that we would pass a small village where he had once lived and his direct descendants lived still. He seemed to have an intergenerational connection with that locality, as if he could feel the Spirit of many generations most readily in the place of his roots. When we were about a kilometer away, we came upon a motorist standing next to his stalled automobile. Mandaza advised his son to stop the car and offer the man assistance. Apparently, the man had run out of gas while on his way to the same village, and he gratefully hopped aboard.

As we resumed our approach to Mandaza's home community, he said that sometimes upon arriving there he would feel the wind of his ancestors' presence as he got out of the car. And just as we arrived and our passenger was disembarking, the largest whirlwind I have ever seen passed by immediately in front of our car—what at home we would call a level-1 tornado!

Nothing was said. We all just looked at each other with approving smiles and accepted the acknowledgment of the old ones and resumed our trip.

In due time, we arrived at our destination, and Mandaza, Israel, and I did hike to the hilltop where the ruined city of Great Zimbabwe had been. Our intention was to commune with the ancestors of many ages. There, by a series of spirit-guided connections, we learned of a powerful traditional healer, Me Furisai. Without hesitation, the three of us set out in our four-wheel drive to find Me Furisai at his remote home isolated atop a hill far from any community. While unknown to Mandaza, in that region near Lake Kyle this shaman was widely known for his eerie deportment and for his ability to enter into deep trances.

After following roadways that became pathways, and then simply with the guiding words of local people, we hiked through the forest to a bare hilltop where we approached the entrance to Me Furisai's hut—his rondavel. Immediately recognizing Mandaza as a traditional healer, he quietly welcomed us into his abode. We descended into a supplicant pose, on our hands and knees, and entered over the customary cow-dung floor while respectfully clapping our tilted hands silently in respect.

Regionally, Me Furisai is respected for his ability to enter the dream world, where he can detect and address spirit (*gombwa*) blockages. According to Shona medicine, such blockages, when the energy of spirit has stopped moving within a person, are the cause of all illnesses.

Right away, Me Furisai enjoined us to snort black tobacco with him, which is one way he enters a trance. The altered state would allow him to meet all our ancestors and so provide him with a deeper introduction to us—sort of like a background check. Immediately upon doing so, he started to become trance possessed; his eyes rolled back, there was a qualitative shift in his voice, and his social self quickly dissolved, melting away into another world. Now powerful and gravelly sounds filled the rondavel—"Yowhey! Wheeoosh!"—exhaled utterances that would frighten most people unfamiliar with this type of ritual. Then the elder spirits, including the spirit of Lion (*mhondoro*), informed him of his guests and gave assurances regarding the purity of our intentions. We were cleared.

After an intense half hour, and much to our surprise, the dramatic ritual was interrupted by the sound of a cell phone ringing behind Me Fursai. Still in trance and confused by the unsettling noise, he slammed his fist onto the phone, putting an end to the sound with which mhondoro was unfamiliar. We learned afterward that a previous cell phone had met a similar demise under the same circumstances.

Me Furisai was continuously inhaling a copious amount of tobacco, so much so that after he was deep in trance and enjoined with the spirit, thick, black streams of mucous were flowing from his nose and over his lips and onto his chin. Since Me Furisai was unaware of what was happening in his immediate environment, Mandaza took out a cloth and attended to the man, gently wiping his face clean, desiring to preserve his rightful dignity in front of us, exemplifying the *I Am*.

Then, while still in trance and with my acquiescence, Me Furisai straddled me, forcefully burrowing the top of his forehead into my body, from my toes to my face, in the process of cleansing me of old residual energies. Later, Mandaza told me that the convening elder spirits had informed Me Furisai that, although I was relatively healthy, my life was still stained with the blood from atrocities once committed against my bloodline ancestors. I concluded that he was referring to the historical attempted genocide of my Acadian relatives after their settlement—and later expulsion—hundreds of years ago from what is now known as Nova Scotia, Canada.

Following another individual cleansing ceremony, this time for Mandaza, the three of us imbibed tobacco water from a common bowl. After sprays of Me Furisai's sputum covered our entire bodies (an African blessing), Mandaza, in reciprocity, offered to conduct a similar ceremony for Me Furisai. The cleansings were intended to open blockages and facilitate a movement of energy in each of us. They were intended to heal ancient family wounds, thereby making us stronger and better able to care for others.

In a generous measure of further respect, Mandaza asked for a bowl of fresh water with which he tenderly washed the feet, and then the hands, of the healer. Eventually, after Me Furisai was no longer surrounded by spirit, he exited the trance and collapsed on his back in exhaustion. His recently ferocious face and vocalizations immediately quieted, and his boyish, smiling face returned. He appeared to be appreciative, renewed, and refreshed. We had been strangers before our arrival but now were enjoined in our shared healing endeavors. Certainly, Mandaza and Me Furisai will meet again, brothers that they are, and together heal many people.

It is a responsibility, as well as an honor, for healers to heal healers. It goes with the territory. To maintain strength in serving the community of humankind, all of us need to participate in periodic cleansing and renewal rituals grounded in love. In this way, there are fewer impediments to the *I Am* state.

Upon observing Mandaza in our times together, I sense that he is endlessly reinvigorated by the love he receives from friends and strangers and every bit as much by the love he gives. He stands on the shoulders of many ancestors who provide humble strength and enduring gratitude. They enter his body through the dream world and become allies, helping Mandaza to minister to others with joy. And any illness, according to Mandaza, embodies sacred teachings. On this my most recent sojourn to Africa, I was privileged to witness the concept of *I Am* move from philosophy to expression. Like illness, this positive spirit is contagious.

The Ancient Maya Symphony

Over the last three years, I have traveled to Guatemala to learn about the Maya people and their cosmology and ceremonially based healing. It is a world of living magic. Mayan cosmology, as reflected in their temples, ancient art, hieroglyphics, and oral history, entails a mathematical understanding of the universe. The heavens guide life in ways that were discovered at least three thousand years ago. This culture extends into Mexico and Honduras, but Guatemala, the population of which is predominantly Mayan, seems to be at the center of this ongoing civilization.

In many ways, the people of this ancient culture remind me of the Shona in that they believe that most illnesses are mental. The brain is the manager of all other body parts. Consequently, the brain must be maintained by sacred principles and a harmonizing way of being in the world. The art of shamans, whether in Africa or North America, seems to be that of convincing, a way of working with the healing power of belief and faith. On a larger scale, Mayan cosmology suggests that we are—much as the Ojibwa of North American would say—on a continuous Healing Path of soul evolution. We must numerically calculate our location on a highly personalized level and develop ourselves in an effort to tug the world forward evolutionarily. For example, by using a complex energy table that coincides with a person's birthdate, the Maya can begin to compute who a person is in terms of personality and life function and what the person's prophecy is. It is a way to access a memory of the future in circular time. Much as Mandaza Kandemwa does, the Maya believe that our relationship with Nature is quintessential in this process.

While in the Tecpan and Chichicastenango regions, I have spent time in ceremony with two Mayan shamans, Victoria Murcielago and Sebastian Panjoj. Victoria is in her thirties and considered a *daykeeper* (a diviner who works with the divinatory calendars; Victoria uses three) and a ceremonialist. Sebastian is at least seventy years old and is referred to as a *principal* by his people; he, too, is a diviner who uses mathematical computation to know and treat his patients. They are always moving energy forces. And as is true in so many other cultures, nothing is done without first calling upon the ancestors.

To understand the Maya, one must appreciate their sweeping, impressive experiment with interpreting the grand laws of the universe. Atop their pyramidal temples in Central America, from around fifteen hundred to three thousand years ago their mystics studied and recorded the daily cycles of life and patterns that the world has followed for millennia, likely forever.

The Mayan astronomers were mathematical philosophers who worked with interlinked calendars, cycles, and energy forces that together impact every individual in the microcosm, while simultaneously being influenced by the macrocosm. In this worldview, to be egotistical is an incredibly narrow and naïve perspective. The unified whole is emphasized. This universe is described as an enormously large and very harmonized symphony.

Contemporary Maya are committed to carrying these old beliefs forward. The Mayan spiritual way of seeing is mathematical at its base, very ordered, and timeless in its origins—and during their rituals it feels magical. The following story will give you an idea of what I mean.

A few years ago, I was blessed to have a friendship with an elderly woman in Des Moines, Iowa, who was a renowned healing-touch practitioner and healer. In her late eighties and in declining health, this friend was someone of whom I had spoken highly to the Mayan shaman Victoria on many occasions. Victoria asked me to provide numerical information pertaining to my friend. She computed that of the twenty prophetic signs, mine was that of a 5-Tijax and my friend's of a 13-Tijax. In Mayan culture, this meant that we were both destined to be powerful healers, with my Des Moines elder being as advanced in that role as almost anyone is.

One of my tasks as a Tijax is to assist in the transformation of another Tijax into the next realm of existence at the time of death. Even though Victoria and my friend were in different countries, Victoria knew of my friend's impending death—not only because I had mentioned that she was seriously ill, but also because Victoria had been computing mathematically determined "energy portals" of that point in time. So, when Victoria emailed me saying that my friend was about to die on or around September 14, it was my duty to go to a place of fire and water to help transport the soon-to-be deceased to the next dimension. I arrived in Guatemala City the September 13, slept for a few hours, and awakened to find an email from Des Moines indicating that my Tijax friend had passed very early in the morning of the 14th.

Off Victoria and I went to Lake Atitlan, where we conducted multiple fire ceremonies below a volcano. Many colorful wax candles were added to the fire on an altar we had erected. As the activities came to end and the fire burned down, the wind suddenly shifted 180 degrees and leaves fell from the tree above us—signs that my Tijax friend had moved on. When the candle wax hardened, I noticed that a gray pool had separated from the other colors and drained off the ceremonial altar onto the ground. The other colors, meanwhile, swirled together in a separate, beautiful pool and remained atop the altar. Thus, an earthly stay had ended and a more beautiful existence was foreseen. Seeing my look of disbelief over what had just transpired, Victoria said to me, "Gerry, that's the way of it."

What she meant is that all events are connected and meaningful; nothing is random. The Maya recognize few separations dividing anything or anyone on this planet, or in all the related universes. In their view, worlds that seem apart are really joined together by invisible threads of energy. Everything on this planet is born of the same energy and carries the vibrations emanating from the original Source, albeit in variants from subtle to bold. What unites everything that can be seen or imagined is like stardust. This creative force originates in distant locations but divinely manifests itself in humans wherever they may be found.

Recognizing that time and distance do not really separate us from the creative force, the Maya believe us to be cocreators of the unfolding evolution of all life forms. History is not the "past";

FIGURE 10. Victoria, the Maya Shaman, Lake Atitlan, Guatemala. Female shamans don't want their faces photographed, especially at ceremonies. (Author's photograph)

it is alive in this moment of *deep time*, evolving and being cocreated with the help of humans. And the universe is not yet complete, any more than we are. Everything and everyone are becoming a new creation.

Mayan cosmology recognizes a grand plan informed by a grand intelligence. Humans are said to be at the center of the universe, not in any egotistical sense but in a way that suggests that we are responsible for furthering creation as it is an unending process. The infinite and eternal intelligence that comprises the cosmos informs us, the human mind serving as a transducer that draws down information from remote and vague frequencies and incorporates consciousness from the distant and faint One Consciousness of the universe. Energetically linked to this larger way of thinking, we are behooved to overcome any notions of a sovereign mind or autonomous existence. Everything is bound together in an immense, far-reaching, single life. As this truth comes to be understood, it is regarded as a soul-awakening, or what some have called *divine audacity*.

Blending in with the ongoing and circular forces of the universe, our vital impulse of being a channel for universal consciousness keeps the past awake inside us, ensuring a harmonized existence today while holding the promise of an even better future. Because we don't resist this higher ordering of the universe, of which we are a small but integral part, we avert many illnesses, psychological and physical. And, in our participating submission to this higher order, the soul is like a seed we lovingly tend until its husk is shed. Our soul awakens and blossoms and we become a full human being in the cycle of life—fulfilling our earthly duty and opening us to the next task of our external existence.

To best understand this celestial philosophy, we must quiet ourselves, meditate as if we are atop a Mayan temple at night, temporarily lose ourselves, and suspend believing in the selfish wants of our clamoring ego. We are challenged to move beyond an individual consciousness to a universal consciousness. This takes us far beyond ego and any personal earthly memory. Paradoxically, we are not only tiny specks; but we are also central figures in this cosmos. We are the evolving cosmos in one of its countless manifestations.

The memory of the universe is encoded in each person, the Maya believe. We are shaped in the form of the cosmos. One goal is to decode its mysteries. Another goal is to vibrate in harmony with the larger cosmic dance that exists beyond this tiny planet. We are energetically linked to this much larger and older way of being and behooved to overcome any notions of an independent mind or independent existence. Much of this state of being can be fostered in age-old ceremonies and rituals that evoke ancient, deeper truths. Ritual helps us in this task by remembering for us. Enacting a ritual within a ceremony awakens genetically transmitted information. It can transport participants to another time, another mind, and other dimensions. Ritual components have three facets that include knowledge or wisdom, sacred elements, and artistic expression. Beauty and sweetness always find their way into all ceremonial rituals.

The Mayan cosmovision with its related values of land stewardship can be understood quite well using the words of the esteemed naturalist John Muir: "If we try to pick out anything by itself, we find it hitched to everything else in the universe."[2] It is reflected as well in the Muslim concepts of surrender and remembrance to far greater, eternal forces. Allah's law also recognizes a transcendent intelligence in the cosmos. Similarly to the Mayan world view, Muslims contend that individuals and tribes must be part of an organic whole with a responsibility to evolve into a higher and more unified level. And in Sufism, the mystical branch of Islam, individuals are really the collective essence of the Divine that guides and directs us. We must, as Quakers suggest, quietly listen for her still small voice within us.

Mayan Meaning, Purpose, and Sense of Our Script at Birth

On what appears a more personal level, in Mayan belief each human packet of the universal energy (appearing as matter) is preordained by cosmological conditions to have a purpose in our collective existence. This energy is our essence, our breath soul, or, as Mayan daykeepers refer to it, our *nawal*. The nawal can also be understood as forces of Nature that preside over our destiny. The complicated Mayan calendars and energies unlock the mystery of who we are and who we have yet to become based on the precise day a person is born. Mayan shamans and daykeepers are in the role of interpreting a person's destiny. Using mathematic charts and computations, as well as crystals and beans, their divinations help unravel the purpose and meaning of life.

Guardian animals can also be regarded as nawals, or universal energy. Primatologist Jane Goodall, from her decades-long observations of chimpanzees, is humbled by the intelligence of instincts and the awe for Nature that our close relative displays. A chimp can sit by a waterfall and be transfixed by what it is observing, just as a person might be. It may be that all creatures are operating from the same playbook, the same manual authored by ancient wisdom. So, it is probable that all animals as well as elements in Nature—water, fire, air, and earth—carry knowledge that awaits our inquiry.

FIGURE 11. Jaguar. Usually a nocturnal animal, Jaguar's powerful spirit offers protection and fierce strength when it appears during soul-retrieval ceremonies. (Author's photograph)

The Maya believe that one task of humans, while in this incarnation, is to exert an influence on their animal potential to bring about an even greater energy for good, especially in terms of communal and worldly benefit. They are encouraged to transcend their seemingly individual selves, realize their collective relationship with every part of Creation, and comprehend and appreciate an ever-expanding sense of family. This is a soul-making process that can take time. But the Maya certainly know there is time aplenty. So, in a gentle and respectful way, they suggest that it matters not *where* a person is on the Healing Path; instead, what truly matters is that the person *is* on the Healing Path—always striving, always becoming.

The Scientific and the Spiritual

Science is based on new discoveries, always moving past the old. Mayan culture is about old discoveries that have stood the test of time. They are evidence-based ways of personal divination and mathematic formulations that can maintain a harmonic world and, therefore, a healthy personal existence in the current reality. As Mayan healers view the history of their people, they see that they have endured wars and turbulence again and again. They believe that those who have survived great hardship over the last two thousand years, extending into recent political attempts at genocide, have their traditions to thank. Therein seems proof that, for those who follow these ancient traditions, a long and peaceful life is assured. This is the crux of their belief system.

Spiritual seekers everywhere attempt to grasp the greater meaning of life and existence. While the Maya use a somewhat scientific and mathematical set of formulas to predict events, they, like Einstein, recognize the importance of adding the spiritual dimension to life's equation. Also, Mayan shamans realize that there is an art to prognosticating. Recognizing a person's origins, current location, and exploration of new dimensions, and by looking ahead to his "death" (meaning his departure from this energetic location), the shaman can develop an understanding of the person's purpose in this realm. As our illusory, material appearance comes to an end, behind the curtain of death (or even nearing it) elements of an evolving soul can be discovered. Death brings us closer to the feelings of unity and love that everyone seeks.

In Mayan culture, responsibility to the community is highly valued, far more than individual advancement. While envy, jealousy, and the pursuit of money is prevalent, the ancient values still clamor to be heard. And it is the priestly shamans who are in the role of keeping these primeval values alive.

Above all else, the Maya believe that everyone must work to sustain and improve *all* of life as it constantly advances itself into more evolved and sophisticated forms. While we exist in this temporary, incarnated fashion, attention must be paid to our transmutation into the next form; it is our eternally sacred responsibility to improve ourselves. All people, as energy carriers, are continuously challenged in this inborn way to advance toward other dimensions that are hidden to us now beyond what we think of as reality. And, as we develop, the universe gets tugged along with us. In this way, as integral parts of an expansive universe, our personal advancement slightly remodels Nature.

Recovering the Ancient Mind

Whether on the African continent or in the highlands of Guatemala, some basic principles of the universe have never been forgotten by tribal peoples. A small number of authentic shamans, usually elders, are the carriers of this sacrosanct knowledge. They are the embodiment of principles noting the importance of connectivity and unity among people and other life forms. They also understand and deeply remember (as in a felt, *intuited* memory) the reciprocal relationship we must have with our life-sustaining environment.

Common to most indigenous cultures is an understanding of the many forms of collective memory, including an aspect of unconsciousness that extends far beyond any individual. This unconsciousness—or perhaps "faint consciousness"—can be considered sacred in that its promptings may be understood as downloads from some sort of illumined mind, supermind, or overmind reflecting the deepest-known awareness of the universe that is constantly being emitted. It is a nondual kind of inner knowing that we all share. In some respects, it can be seen as our soul, our original form, and our essence that is shared with everything in various forms of life's manifestation. The physicist Erwin Schröedinger has said: "Consciousness is a singular of which the plural is unknown. There is only one thing and that which seems to be a plurality is merely a series of different aspects of this one thing, produced by a deception, the Indian maya, as in a gallery of mirrors."[3] In other words, we need to get out of our limiting paradigm of self. Most people in modern cultures rarely reflect on sources of thought that are so nonlocal and mystical in Nature, and thus they forget our place in the grand scheme of things.

Contributing to this amnesia are scientific and technological forces that think for us. But the universe extends far beyond the limits of our technological instruments of measure and our remaining senses. Ask any real shaman. For example, shamans everywhere rarely are limited to the mere five senses to which modern science ascribes us. All of them are great at intuiting. Many traditional cultures communicate nonlocally, or to ancestors who have passed over.

The Mayoruna of the Peruvian Amazon, for instance, practice thought exchange without verbalization, writing, or hand signs; I call it *beaming*. They can receive messages in mental pictures. The Kogi of Colombia have an alternate form of communication that has been described as silent speech. And without a written language, let alone computers, they have long maintained their astonishing ability for long-term memory, including of the beginning of time and the rampage the conquistadors brought to their region in 1498.[4]

Other isolated indigenous groups of the Amazon can visually look into another person's body to diagnose medical problems. Amazonian tribes commonly shapeshift into the spirit of the jaguar; the Shona of Africa commonly merge their spirits with those of leopards and lions. Elderly women healers of the Inupiat First Nation along the Arctic coast can diagnose internal illnesses and injuries with the "eyes" of their hands—a form of synesthesia. The Q'ero of the Andes can see energetic auroras surrounding people and stars during daylight hours. Hadza Bushmen of Tanzania "wire" messages without cables or phones. Many groups have enhanced vision, including night vision and an acute depth of visual perception far beyond that known in the Western world. Enhanced hearing and taste and a clairvoyant sense have been documented among the Huni Kuin of the Upper Amazon. Some cultures report shared consciousness and group visions and have internal compasses that orient them in an uncannily accurate fashion. The Shipibo of Peru, and many other indigenous groups, speak of plant communication. They learn from plant life just what mixtures will work together to produce a desired medicinal result—concoctions that would otherwise take millions of trial-and-error tests to determine when such luxury of time and research is impossible amid the harsh restrictions of jungle life.

Eden Phillpotts once wrote, "The world is full of magic things, potentially waiting for our senses to grow sharper."[5] I believe he was referring to the atrophy of our senses that need to be sharpened once again. Some of these magical, mysterious, invisible, and, I believe, nascent abilities await our rediscovery. However, research into the many near-extinct senses is regarded not as a serious scientific endeavor but simply as a curiosity. Too frequently, such talents are met with complete disbelief by academics who have little if any experience with indigenous cultures or who personally have never known sensory perceptions beyond rudimentary touch, taste, hearing, sight, and smell—and then only within our current measurement ranges. Other doctrinaire scholars, with limited or no field experience among remote cultures, write off reports of their enhanced sensory abilities as being delusions or drug-induced hallucinations by unscholarly primitive peoples.

In "civilized" cultures, the aforementioned talents, deep remembrances, open-minded thinking, and direct spiritual experiences have significantly atrophied from inactivity. For example, Joseph Chilton Pearce, in *The Biology of Transcendence,* cites studies that reveal a dramatic decline in the human ability to distinguish sounds—dropping from three hundred thousand to one hundred thousand discernable sounds over a fifteen-year period. He also noted that thirty years ago the average person could detect 350 different shades of a particular color, while today the number has plummeted to 130.[6]

The studies Pearce mentions had been conducted by the University of Tubingen, in Germany, contrasting the "highly literate" countries of Europe and the United States with so-called primitive groups in Guatemala and other unnamed locations. Notably, the children from the primitive settings, many of whom were classified as preliterate, showed greater levels of sensory sensitivity (25–30 percent) than those of industrial/technological countries.[7]

Yet, along with many philosophers, anthropologists, and systems scientists, I contend that these latent or atrophied sensory abilities are still written into our basic code. Jung referred to the hiding spot as being the *collective unconscious*. Spiritual seekers everywhere are trying to resurrect the deep sense of the invisible universe and the sense of unity it affords them. In this way, as psychiatrist Kurt Goldstein said before Maslow, we can self-actualize, get a grasp of the real world, and reach our full potential.[8]

We are beginning to recognize that something primal is missing from our inner lives. We mistakenly believe it resides outside us. So, we travel great distances to do some spiritual window shopping. Many people travel great distances to find something miraculous that is believed to exist outside themselves. But Nature is not outside us. She permeates our very being. We are not disconnected. Many seekers experiment with plant medicines such as ayahuasca, San Pedro, iboga, and psilocybin, or the hallucinogenic venom of jungle toads. Travelers can enter altered states by participating in dramatic indigenous ceremonies. I do not mean to say that these activities are inherently bad or wrong. They may be better understood as the canary in the coal mine, a signal of a hankering that is going on deep inside us. It is like a primordial yearning that can no longer go unnoticed, because the very survival of human life on this planet is contingent upon the deeper awareness of our oneness with Nature.

Sometimes poetry says things best. I am reminded of the poem written by Jane Goodall when she was a student many decades ago:

The Old Wisdom

When the night wind makes the pine trees creak
And the pale clouds glide across the dark sky,
Go out, my child, go out and seek
Your soul: the Eternal I.

For all the grasses rustling at your feet
And every flaming star that glitters high
Above you, close up and meet
In you: the Eternal I.

Yes, my child, go out into the world; walk slow
And silent, comprehending all, and by
Your soul, the Universe, will know
Itself: the Eternal I.

To heal people, the importance of "dying to ego" or self-importance, while unifying harmoniously with the Great Mystery, is the central message of shamanism everywhere.

Healing Practices in
Shamanism Worldwide

I have been a slow learner. As Mtshali, the Zulu healer, strongly suggested, it might take a spiritual two-by-four, gently applied to the head, to awaken me to the ways of the sangoma. Nothing subtle would work with me. And, he further reasoned, much more direct personal experience would be necessary before real learning would occur and become embedded in my psyche. His wisdom has been proven true, again and again, as I have supplanted constricted academic facts and blind faith with the expansive, direct experience of the mystery world. Now I am committed to bridging the old and the new, bringing the best of both worlds of professional psychology and medicine together, to promote harmony and, therefore, optimal health.

My indigenous mentors, along with expanded experience from a much wider world than I had previously known, have raised my awareness of some of the central concepts and values that form the heart of traditional healing practices. I will explore a few of them.

Sacred Magic

It was in an undergraduate anthropology course that I was introduced to some of the theories of Bronislaw Malinowski, widely regarded as the father of social anthropology. I learned that where there is illness and fear, yet hope, a belief in magic often is required to change the course of events.

By *magic*, I mean an outcome that appears mysteriously, not based on reason or scientific knowledge. More than just superstition or nonsense, *magic* as I regard it is deeply tied to belief and religion, what is called *magico-religious* thinking. Magical events typically occur without any process of cause and effect that we can yet understand; and, when we don't fully understand cause and effect, the circumstance will feel mysterious, if not dubious. What seems magical is often, however, the forerunner of a science to be. When a medicine for an illness has not been developed, the ability of the mind to activate physiological change is often beyond our comprehension, so we call the outcome, whether positive or negative, *magical*.

Magic in the sense in which I describe it serves a powerful healing function. When it is embedded in reverent rituals and participatory communal ceremonies, the acts become imbued with *super natural* powers born of the human mind. With magic—born in the imagination of the mind and the mystery of the world all around us—we are opened to boundless possibilities. It bridges a gap between what we know and what we have yet fully to master. The myth and art of magic must have a societal pedigree. Its traditional integrity across generations not only preserves its power, but, with the passage of time, strengthens it. Long-held beliefs and sacred rituals give it even more legitimacy, more efficacy.

Magic is not something separate from us. We are hardwired with a mysterious inner healer—evolutionary software—that when sufficiently stimulated through dramatic ceremonies invigorates restorative changes inside us. Slumbering within each of us is a higher organizing intelligence that most of humanity has intellectually forgotten over millennia. It turns out that we are far more gifted than we assume. This is one of the insights to be gleaned from being in the company of reverent indigenous healers. A dramatic alteration of our personal frequency, what can be regarded as our vibration, can awaken the doctor residing in us. That is what I mean by *sacred* magic. It is a science touched with an invisible spirit and the potentiating power of community. It is what was once called *primitive science* and now respectfully referred to as *jungle medicine*. This was the power that invigorated Juan Fidel's healing (see chapter 2), which relied, in part, on the placebo effect.

Fortunately, science is now opening to the study of this placebo response and is taking it more seriously. It is an inquiry into the faith in faith and the study of belief systems and their relationship to hope and suggestion that gives impetus to the healing process. What was once wrongly branded as quackery is now used to enhance the effectiveness of pharmaceuticals, particularly antidepressants. Even sham surgeries have been found to be as effective as traditional operations, from the knees to the heart.

Shamans are notorious for their dramatic performances, the use of sleight-of-hand techniques, trickery, and chicanery, but their intentions must be pure and clean. Their goal is to heal, and if some showmanship enhances suggestions and raises expectations, then so be it. Plato informed us that everything that deceives may also be said to enchant; there are two sides to almost everything. Yet, as Hippocrates cautioned us, "First, do no harm." It isn't uncommon for a shaman, wanting what is best for the patient, to acknowledge his limitations (e.g., setting a bone) and refer a patient to a Western physician.

Humility

My observations of numerous shamans from around the world has revealed one universal quality among the best of them—humility, especially when it is combined with an authoritative demeanor. Deep down, all traditional healers recognize that the doctor never cures a patient; patients cure themselves. The shaman fills the role of a carpenter of rituals and the choreographer of ceremonies that remove barriers to healing. Recall Juan Fidel, whose fear of death was an obstruction to healing. Once removed, he was restored to health.

Not long ago, a trauma patient came to me for care after several decades of discounting emotional abuse by her husband in what was essentially a form of soul theft. As a result of this abuse, she had become very deferential to men and unable to trust her own inner guidance. During one of our sessions together, she brought up concerns about her recent ankle replacement. She was an unassuming individual who had spent several preop therapy sessions releasing fears of the procedure, the aging process, and the possibility of her immobilization in the years to come. This woman worked hard to address her own obstacles to self-healing well before the surgery. After surgery, she immediately invited a friend to the hospital to employ energy movement and healing-touch treatments to assist her recovery from anesthesia and to awaken and reinvigorate internal healing powers. These treatments were intended to reset her body after the bodily trauma of anesthesia and surgery, and she regarded them as being very helpful. Her enthusiasm was shared with the surgeon.

Later, she told me that her surgeon discounted her testimony and immediately exhibited X-rays of the reconstruction. He seemed quite proud, she said, appearing to be more interested in giving himself accolades for his carpentry skills than in asking her how she could be playing an active part in her recovery. The physician's demeanor reminded my patient of her abusive ex-husband, who had been diagnosed as having a narcissistic personality disorder. Much to her credit, she surmised that exclusively relying on her doctor for healing would not be good enough. A modest but firm respect for her internal restorative processes was a necessary adjunct to the skills of her surgeon.

Paradoxically, an authentic shaman rarely introduces himself as a shaman. Men such as Mandaza Kandemwa and P. H. Mtshali are aware of the immense powers with which they cooperate in healing ceremonies. I have come to know true shamans who recognize that the powers that accompany them—the powers that promote dramatic and spontaneous healings—do not arise from within them. Traditional healers are but conduits, who, like orchestra leaders, conduct a harmonizing ceremony that has many contributing components. They take a back seat to powers that the patient carries or that are attributed to the spirit world, including deceased ancestors whose presence is invoked by prayer or during a trance just before the rituals commence. As I observed them, both Mandaza and Mtshali were humbled before the spirits and were deferential toward them.

As I recount in chapter 1, I learned from Mandaza—who sat me down by a tree to ask of it, "How might I serve you"—that

I was not here on Earth to build a career or a reputation; nor was my healing practice to be centered around the accumulation of money or possessions. The mantra Mandaza lives by is one of service. Ego, which can serve many healthy functions, is to be carefully observed and restrained. I am reminded of the surprisingly humble Muhammad Ali, whose late-life evolution in rhetoric went from "Me? Whee!" to "Me. We!" as his affliction with Parkinson's disease swallowed some of his early pride. Ali was humbled in the knowledge that he needed others, and his elder years were focused almost entirely on service to others.

I recall sitting with Mandaza on a winter day in Zimbabwe. As he spoke to me about this topic of humility, I was transfixed by his quiet presence. Mandaza's words were heartfelt. And then, Nature flew in to add an exclamation mark: a white Zimbabwean dove descended into his healing hut and landed on his shoulder! It was as if his frequency, his vibration, felt safe and inviting to the dove. Moved and humbled myself, I began to speak of similar themes of humility and service. Just then, a second dove flew in and landed atop *my* head! Without that kind of direct experience, I would likely not have remembered the poignancy of his words on that day. I had been struck by another sacred two by four. Nature was directing me to pay attention.

In this age of narcissism in the United States, psychologists and physicians often construct websites to promote themselves, market their service, and ultimately to prosper personally. Many contemporary healers, in their business and personal life, spend significant amount of time on Facebook crafting an appealing image of themselves. "Likes" have become very important currency, both to individuals and to corporations. Often this marketing is reflective of a personal need for affirmation and professional advancement. Today's healers often fail to recognize the anomic features of this competitive trend.

Indigenous healers remind us to return to the core ideals of the earliest medicine, the deepest values that must remain at the foundation of traditional medicine. As Kurt Anderson wrote in a 2017 article in *The Atlantic,* "We may be humbled to one day find ourselves joined, across the distance of stars, to a more ancient web of mind."[1] And, in the recognition of our interconnectedness, we can move to the idea of the One Mind; seeing our completeness comes with an awareness of the Whole.

Full, Attentive Presence

The most effective and reverent shamans have a remarkable ability to stay focused on their patient, in some cases all night long in an ayahuasca ceremony, or for days throughout a traditional Navajo healing. The character of Western medicine reflects its existence in our distracted modern culture. The standard practice is to multitask from the beginning to the end of the day. Quantity has overtaken quality in most area of our lives, and the healing profession is not an exception. As Maggie Jackson warns us in her book, *Distracted,* our society is on the verge of losing the capacity for deep, sustained focus. She suggests that we are slipping toward another dark age—ominously, an age when our marvelous technologies and high-tech connectivity will nevertheless engender shallow and inattentive relationships, and a loneliness and despair, that no gadgetry can ameliorate. What was intended to bring us together is causing us to drift apart.[2]

Virtual and simulated realities, while providing treasured altered states, entertain us but do not assuage our growing loneliness and alienation. Cyberspace has become a consensual hallucination. When connecting online, we get little more than a diluted and condensed version of the person with whom we are communicating, and we usually miss out on extended face-to-face contact. With the speed of technology our acquaintances are "right there" yet while not being present. Virtual reality is fast becoming the preferred reality, for socializing and even sex. As the Ju/'hoansi Bushmen repeatedly say in the 2016 film documentary *Ghostland*, after being plucked out of Namibia and dropped into a large German city, "This is mad." Western urban life was anything but natural to them and certainly not very appealing.

Without eye-to-eye closeness, without the activation of our mirror neurons, we literally lose the ability to read human emotions in others. In actual relationships, mirror neurons don't just help you *imagine* how it feels to be intimate; they literally put you through the paces, neurologically and biochemically. Technology, in contrast, generates a pseudo-psychopathy brought on by pixelated miniature images on a computer screen that does not foster real intimacy. Instead, amped up intensity—extreme pleasure matched with extreme excitement, which is the perfect recipe for addiction—has become our way of self-comforting. Intensity is replacing intimacy. Human beings are losing the ability to compete successfully with the novelty and immediate rewards in our wired age. It may be that the large number of men who are turning to computer sex over real-time sex are doing so because real life simply can't begin to compete with the repeated dopamine spritzes on our brains that technology affords. Besides, real sex requires a more substantial investment of time.

Today's distracted brains must be amped up to detect emotions and feel pleasure. Subtle factors such as facial nuances are increasingly lost on us. The result can be snap judgments followed by terse and insensitive tweets.

Susan Pinker, in *The Village Effect*, sees the trend. She believes that the meaning of the term *social network* has morphed into connoting the ways our machines are connected. As an increasingly lonely people, we are losing vital connections, and, with them, our natural ways of healing.[3] It is as if digital natives are saying to each other, "I want to put my head on your shoulder, but don't stand so close to me. Please, no oxytocin. Minimal eye contact is preferred. I want to get back to my screen." But without the benefits of our natural bonding chemicals and the connections that arise with the activation of our mirror neurons, we are losing the ability to develop and maintain secure attachments. As I write this segment, I can look over my right shoulder and see a large photo mounted on my wall. It is of a Hadza mother and her child, bound together with a swaddling cloth, faces only inches apart, hands exploring each other's faces, both glowing in contentment (see ch. 4, fig. 6). As my Tanzanian guide, Kambona, said to me, "The old is gold."

To get below the surface of a patient's illness requires a laser-like ability to focus without being distracted. When shamans engage in their art, they often note that "the problem is not the problem." What starts out looking like an intestinal problem or body aches may more fully addressed at its core as disharmony— and not just disharmony at home or in close relationships, but falling out of balance and losing connection with all the relatives of the world, no matter how animated the patient appears.

Even in a remote Venda community in South Africa, technology is encroaching. A friend who believed his courage and confidence was slipping away requested a scarification ceremony to regain personal strength. Standing outside his rondavel, the shaman, with a razor blade in hand, was making parallel cuts in the patient's shoulder. To stay calm, my friend tried to stare at a distant object while keeping his breath slow and rhythmic. I could see, however, that his level of tension remained high. Then, midway through the procedure, the shaman's cell phone rang, startling us all. The shaman placed the razor blade on some dusty bricks, took the call, and socialized with an acquaintance for several minutes. After hanging up and without any segue, he resumed cutting with the unsterilized blade. From this example, you can appreciate that indigenous ways aren't without some of the same societal influences we face. Traditional healers may not be perfectly focused at all times and don't always lend themselves to romantic idealization. Sometimes shamans, too, need to silence their phones and perform one task at a time.

Under a cultural steamroller of words, the restorative power of silence is often lost. Sitting quietly in the full awareness of another can be very stabilizing and health invoking. With no phone ringing or email pings, but instead holding single-pointed attention on a suffering individual, a satisfying connection is felt. Quiet moments need not be filled with wise counsel or even the *active listening* proposed by psychotherapist Carl Rogers, characterized by an occasional "I understand" to show attentiveness. Rather, I propose *radical listening*, meaning that the therapist asks the patient to pause for a while as the therapist attempts to discern the meaning in the long, poignant silence. Radical listening is about going behind and beyond the words. In essence, the therapist is saying to the patient, "I will leave my world behind to be present with you." In that way, the patient is deeply heard, validated, and comforted. Sometimes a loving silence is eloquent.

Community

It is nothing short of astonishing to see what authentic human connectivity can do to people. I witnessed the effect firsthand in Nicaragua in 2013 when I was meeting with indigenous healers and teaching at the University of the Coastal Caribbean in Bluefields. The social conditions of the time produced a wave of mass panic (*grisi sikness*), in which dramatic alterations in human behavior were infectiously sweeping from community to community.

The occasion that triggered the situation was the release of public health information, especially among the Miskitu people of Awastara, that awakened many memories of sexual abuse among individuals who had suppressed those memories. With the topic brought so close to the surface of many people's minds, a collective angst and panic unfolded as women began rising up en masse. They were responding to their untreated sexual abuse that, although it wasn't publicly acknowledged, was widespread in the villages. As one person erupted with violent rage, others responded in kind. A cumulative emotional frenzy became rampant for a time until traditional healers were called upon to intervene, employing community rituals as one-on-one efforts were not effective.

In quite a different situation, but following the social contagion model, once when I was in Tanzania I heard about three teenage girls there who began laughing uncontrollably one day. This started an "epidemic" of laughter that spread from community to community, "infecting" over two hundred teenage girls via face-to-face contact. Four schools were closed in three villages before the "disturbance" was quelled and life returned to normal.

So, community has power. Being connected to a tightly connected group of friends is likely to impact your health in countless ways, negative and positive. On a benign level, yawning, scratching, and coughing can be passed from person to person. More significantly, in tight-knit communities longevity is high, the risk of dementia is lower, pain is lessened, inflammation is reduced, recovery from cancer is enhanced, heart attacks are less likely, rates of depression stay low, and even skin abrasions heal faster than among folks who are more solitary and insular. Socially isolated and ostracized people feel their exclusion on a visceral level. When a person experiences sustained isolation, the human brain becomes impaired in ways that are similar to someone who has suffered a traumatic head injury. Married women who are in emotionally abusive relationships have elevated levels of cortisol, along with other neuroendocrine signs of distress.[4]

Both the quantity and quality of communal ties are important. Social interaction is healing. When people come together in groups, as is common in traditional societies, health contagion occurs. As the person targeted for healing improves, others in the circle often show symptom remission from their personal illnesses. Contemporary indigenous healers believe and often assert that for 99 percent of human history we lived in intimate tribal groups of twelve to thirty-six people. It is in close linkage with others that our bodies have developed and shown forward evolution. And naturally, when aboriginal people required medical care, they came together in cohesive groups to lend support to the ailing person.

José Stevens, a modern-day shaman, has noted how groups of people who assemble for a healing create a potentiating response in the patient. In other words, every person added to the ceremony has a multiplying effect. For example, two supporters are said to have the healing energy of four; eight people, of sixty-four, and so on. When many people are lovingly focused on one suffering person, they generate immense energy that can shift a person's vibration in dramatic ways, usually in the direction of health. But the members of the healing circle must commit their time for the duration; they can't bail out early or multitask. Just as importantly, it helps when they are calm, loving, and optimistic and share similar values and beliefs pertaining to health and healing.[5]

Circling up in community can also have prevention benefits. Upon meeting with northern Canadian First-Nation communities, I have learned that some tribal customs encourage a ritual that connects a newborn child to the tribe after the child's umbilical cord has been severed. Shortly after a mother has delivered the baby, a group will gather to create the equivalent of a new umbilical cord of social ties. They convene in a circle and pass the baby clockwise from person to person. (In the northern hemisphere, the sun appears to move clockwise across the sky, which may be why that direction has been deemed the natural and sacred way of doing things.) Each individual meets and greets the infant, forming an important link. Prayers are personally offered to the baby, promising continuing love and protection through health and illness over the lifespan. When one attachment is broken, many others can replace it. In a way, the circle is also good for the persons sitting in it, as the ritual serves as a social glue.

In some regions of rural Guatemala, indigenous Maya save the navel stump—the belly button—after birth and store it in a multigenerational holy bundle. These little balls join hundreds of others dating back many generations, creating a collective memory. The bundle is periodically smudged whenever a major community event occurs. Martin Prechtel, in *Long Life: Honey in the Heart,* has referenced this renewal ritual, referring to the bundle of belly buttons as the "Umbilicus of the House." He likens it to a community's *spiritual DNA* that carries life from generation to generation, maintaining valued ties.[6] In this way, no one ever regards him- or herself as a mere individual.

It has also been documented that, following a Mayan birth, lactating women who want to bless a new mother and child come together and pass the baby from woman to woman. The infant is allowed to suckle from each woman, and, in this deeply intimate way, becomes connected to various clans within a village.[7] Hence the child is embraced by all, related to all. In years to come, disputes can be prevented by reminding one another of how this now-older individual was once suckled by the entire community and so is "one of our own." A peacemaking ritual has been renewed; it is ongoing.

Men, too, can be included in Guatemalan rituals. Prechtel has observed that a child's first item of clothing is made from the father's old clothing. By this means the child will be swaddled in the father's subtle aromas and spirit, thereby not easily forgotten. To further remind a baby of her father, the mother may place one of the father's shirts under the baby as it sleeps. When father is away, perhaps working in the fields, in this comforting and reassuring way a baby can feel the important paternal connection that is continuously alive. The child is not only joined with the father but protected as well, until the father can return to the child's side.[8]

Animal Guides

The figure of an animal guide played a prominent role in a recent spiritual awakening I witnessed during a patient intensive in the mountains of Montana. The experience involved a young man I will call Brent, who was learning to embrace his sexual addiction and all the teachings embedded in it. Brent spent a week of his summer in my company exploring inner parts of his being in the folds of several mountain ranges. During this time, repeated reminders were proffered—in dreams and visions, as well as in verbal communications—that in an intimate connection with Nature the grip of his addiction would begin to relax. I encouraged Brent to seek out a guardian animal during his stay, one whose wisdom and demeanor could offer a subtle form of guidance to complement the more cerebral forms of psychotherapy to which I was also exposing him.

Upon completion of this retreat, Brent was walking down a mountain trail with me while discussing insights of the week. He spoke of having an unhealthy part of himself being washed away. And, as we crossed a creek, he intuitively was guided to shed his clothes, lie down in the cold water, and let its cleansing powers wash over him. Then we continued our trek to the basecamp, where he would humbly enter the sweat lodge and further discard the shame that had served to fuel his addiction. It was midafternoon under a warm sun when we reached the lodge, where a large fire was heating up the grandfathers (rocks). Giving the rocks plenty of time to heat up, we discussed Brent's experiences of the week with the Native American elder who would conduct the sweat.

Brent disclosed his disappointment that the animal (Owl) he had cognitively chosen to be his guardian had never appeared to him during the entire week. We asked if he had spent much time outside during the dark of night to summon Owl. Brent replied that his days were so full and exhausting that all he could do in the evenings was sleep. We further inquired whether he had spoken to Owl at any time over the course of the week, which he quickly dismissed as silly.

A challenge seemed in order. I asked Brent to imagine what it would sound like if he put into words what he wanted from Owl.

He responded by saying, "His presence."

Redirecting him, I said, "Say an invitation now, out loud."

Smiling, as if to suggest that this was a little inane, he spoke to Owl.

We continued talking while going on with our preparation of the sweat lodge.

"What does Owl signify?" Brent asked our Native friend.

Abruptly his elder replied, "Death."

Clearly, Brent was discouraged with that response, as it wasn't as romantic and inspirational as he had hoped.

But the elder went on to clarify by saying, "Death of what, we don't know. Its presence could mark the end of an era in your life, the demise of your addiction only to be replaced by something better. This is West-Window activity, when a goodbye is said to old ways that have not been helpful."

Okay, that information was a bit more encouraging.

Brent continued the discussion of Owl as the grandfather rocks started to pop. And this is where mystery swept in. Right then, in the middle of the afternoon, a great horned owl soared into camp and landed on a fence post just a few yards from the lodge! Owl turned and faced us as if to inquire, "You called?"

This *super natural* event was a very personal exclamation point to end Brent's week of self-examination. I took the liberty of photographing the event to give it lasting influence in Brent's recovery. Owl stuck around long enough to commemorate the event. With its departure, we entered the sweat lodge humbly to give thanks to all the relatives who were assisting in Brent's transformation experience. As the Lakota expression goes, *Mitakayue oyasin*: "All my relations!"

FIGURE 12. Great Horned Owl. Brent's animal guardian appeared just as he summoned it. (Author's photograph)

Revelations and visions of this sort are often regarded as very private; some indigenous people believe that, if they were shared, they would lose their power. So, it is with some alteration of the facts that this otherwise true story is told. It is the kind of direct experience of which Mtshali has spoken. Such events are like a gentle two-by-four to the head that leaves an indelible impression of the benevolent powers found in Nature and in shamanic healing.

Beauty and Harmony

It is difficult to separate beauty and harmony, hard to appreciate the former if the latter isn't felt. When balance and harmony are present in a person's life—in intrapersonal and interpersonal relationships and with all life forms sharing this space on Earth—beautiful things happen, our moods lift, and healing occurs.

And harmony is contagious, just as negativity and disease can be. A Hopi elder named Evelyn once described health to me in tongue-in-cheek fashion. Her reservation is encircled by the larger Navajo reservation and, as is typical in most Native American groups, she uses humor affectionately. When I asked Evelyn to describe health to me, she first gave her interpretation of the Navajo worldview:

"They believe that health results from living in harmony with all the relatives, whether they be plants, animals, or grandfather rocks; they see beauty in all things in the universe."

Then she playfully contrasted that with the broader Hopi worldview by saying, "We, the Hopi, believe that health results from living in harmony with all the relatives, whether they be plants, animals, or grandfather rocks; we see beauty in all things in *all* the universes."

Whether an indigenous culture perceives a single universe or a plurality of them, though, each one I have visited believes that harmony and a recognition of beauty in all things supports health and promotes healing.

In chapter 13, I introduced Victoria Murcielago, a Mayan shaman, ceremonialist, and daykeeper residing in the Guatemalan Highlands with whom I have participated in outdoor fire ceremonies many times. Shamans listen to Nature, as she has a language unto herself. When any human listens to the faint whispers of Nature—something larger than ourselves—creativity arises within us. A creative consciousness is always receptive to mystery, and mystery causes us to listen for the unexpected, the miraculous, and the secrets of Divinity, all of which ultimately fertilize our ongoing emergence. After a few *super natural* events have touched our very core, an *abundance consciousness* develops, in which absolutely anything seems possible. Many priestly shamans wear this realization, and it can be contagious.

Victoria has taught me that healing ceremonies must always occur on a firm foundation. The three bases of the foundation are described as a triangle, much like the similarly shaped volcanic mountains to which her ceremonial grounds are always close.

The first base of the triangular foundation is that every ceremony must include traditional knowledge, whether obtained from mentoring, studying, or arrived at intuitively. With the passage of time, and with accumulated experience, knowledge unfolds into wisdom, and when a healer is grounded in many years of experience that amalgam of information can be applied artfully.

The second base of the triangle involves spirit. The presence of the ancestors and *nawals* (divine energy and guardian spirits) are invoked at the start of every ceremony to honor and mollify them, as well as to invite their assistance. Ceremonies occur at ancient ruins, cities, or other sacred locations that have been used for hundreds if not thousands of years. It is within such an atmosphere of great reverence that cleansing, healing, and growth can take place.

The third base of the triangle is that every ceremony must include art and beauty. The shaman ceremonialist will create a beautiful altar upon which tradition knowledge, sacredness, and artfulness combine to transform the recipient. Creativity arises from a place of joy, and accompanying it is a desire to add beauty and harmony to life. The result is healing.

The beauty of Mayan fire ceremonies reflects the beauty residing in the person for whom the event is being conducted. This, in turn, invites lost beauty—perhaps from a soul loss or soul theft—to be restored. Additionally, another level of beauty

FIGURE 13. A Healing Mandala. The colorful circle of helpful elements adds a touch of beauty to a ceremonial opening. (Author's photograph)

is bestowed on the person who may have been defiled by the profane acts of an abuser. In accordance with a person's nawal, carefully selected items reflecting that beauty and implant ideas of hopefulness will be placed on the circular altar. I have seen shamans use candles of many colors, compressed wood chips infused with *copal* (incense), stick incense, raw brown sugar, herbs (such as basil, cinnamon, or allspice), flowers, cacao, seeds, and nuts.

With such items attractively arranged, and with prayerful words showered over the fire, new associations are being made. Old hurts are now intermixed with sweetness and beauty, creating a new association that allows for a healthy integration of life's pain.

The transformative power of fire in these ceremonies mirrors that of the volcano. Fire ceremonies can cleanse people of old negative energy while lifting them up to a place of peace. The last element of a trauma story can then become the more positive remembrance of this sacred event. Sometimes chocolate is ritually placed on the tongue: I can recall walking away from ceremonies for individuals with a piece of Guatemalan dark chocolate melting in my mouth, much like a communion wafer but without a morbid crucifixion story behind it. In what was similar to the closing of a church ceremony when we are instructed to "go in peace," I felt as if my final message was to "walk in sweetness."

There is an old link between the Mayan culture and the Hopi and Navajo cultures of North America. Upon the completion of a beautiful fire ceremony in Guatemala, I heard words similar to an old Navajo Beauty Path chantway that goes something like this:

There is beauty above me.
There is beauty below me.
I see beauty to my left.
I see beauty to my right.
There is beauty behind me.
I see beauty in front of me.
There is beauty in my heart.
I will walk in beauty this day.

Love

When a person is harmed by cruelty, abuse, or a hex, the cor-ollary may be to add a safe form of loving care and attention. Sacred ceremony assists in the removal of negative energy. It can begin with a sweeping of the body's energy, the sprayed mist of alcohol, the aroma of perfume blown over a person, or the smoke of tobacco enveloping them.

In the United States, with enhanced awareness of the epidemic of sexual and physical abuse, we have veered away from virtu-ally all forms of patient-healer physical contact. Consequently, health-care providers have become extraordinarily cautious to set and maintain physical boundaries with patients who have been victimized in these ways. The result, however, can often result in a clinically cold environment in which technique trumps warmth and compassion.

Love softens the body's armor, the Zulu healer P. H. Mtshali believed (sadly, he passed away in 2011). Suffering that is followed by love, he contended, opens people to the greatest miracles of healing, with the former being as essential as the latter. This influential sangoma helped me understand how health is restored more fully when love is a part of the soul-recovery equation.

To my amazement, while in his eighties Mtshali remained an active member in the Swaziland branch of the Traditional Healers Association. This oversight organization has taken heed of the dangers of unscrupulous healers ("black sangomas") while standing firm in their belief that loving attentiveness plays an integral part in patient healing. Care must be heart driven while professional parameters are respected.

Mtshali's admonition to me on this point was clear. He said, "No person can be cured by a sangoma if they are without love for their patient. Love can cure on its own without the application of any *muti* [medicine]."

This love must start with self-love, he asserted, which entails the clearing of all hatred or animosity within us. "The foremost thing," Mtshali clarified, "is to love your work, as love always creates good results." He believed that when we transmit love during healing it comes back to us; in giving, we receive. Love, by its very definition, constitutes a sacred relationship, and the interpersonally sacred must be incorporated into any human reparative process, especially after patients have experienced the profane.

Highly experienced psychotherapists know this at a gut level. But, as licensed professionals, we fear the loss of reputation if we publicly acknowledge that love plays an important role in the healing arts. In fact, the prevalent mind-set is that love equates to sentimentalism and has no place in the clinical setting of evidence-based treatments. It smacks of unprofessionalism, lacks precision, and certainly is not scientific. Furthermore, some of us react adversely to the display of this most human of traits because of our own unresolved issues. Yet what could be more unprofessional than to treat patients with a string of cold and standardized techniques that fail to respect their innate sacred beauty? *Personhood*, as it has been called, meaning the full presence of our authentic self when alive in both the healer and the patient, can thaw a patient's chronically inflexible and defensive response to what he has experienced in a previously hurtful world. It can make the difference between breaking down and breaking open.

Mahatma Gandhi once asked, "The language of the lips is easily taught, but who can teach the language of the heart?"[9] The longest journey any person can take in a lifetime, especially as an evolving therapist, is to travel the eighteen inches from the head to the heart. Even more broadly, it requires the movement from a personal heart to a global heart. This is our penultimate task as healers.

Conclusion

Albert Einstein repeatedly encouraged us to stay open to the essential roles of spirituality and imagination in developing any new scientific theory. He proclaimed that imagination is more important than knowledge, as the latter is so limited. In fact, imagination reaches beyond the intellect. Einstein warned against the futility of trying to develop new theories with the exact same thinking that had been used before.

Certainly, innovation has its place. But are advancements always built on ideas that only look forward? Intellectual advances often need old as well as new starting points if they are to formulate pioneering perspectives. This is the paradox: in part, the future must be imagined from a perspective that is, importantly, buttressed with old and lasting wisdom. Otherwise, one decade down the road, we may find ourselves in the frustrating dilemma described in a 2011 *Slate* piece that said, "Looking back, the future didn't last long."[1] The future must be erected on solid ground.

For this reason, it is important to remember ancient, time-tested methods of healing. Thinking will not advance significantly if an either/or mentality reigns. It is natural to process information in this dichotomous way, but—dare I say—lazy. To reach outside the proverbial box and enter into unfamiliar terrains of the consciousness, shamans have long sought ways of stretching the mind. This effort often entailed vision quests, ways to expand what we see in this world and reach into other realities for new insights. It could involve fasting, the ingestion of entheogens to alter the limiting day-to-day reality, or pushing the body-mind to extremes through sacred suffering, the Native American Sun Dance being a classic example. In this way, ancient cultures were always trying to expand their horizons and their knowledge of the universe of which they were an integral part.

If we assume that a dog or a cat may be limited to their here-and-now experience of what is immediately before them, and further considering that humans are also animals, could it be, as William James said, that we know little about the larger world we inhabit, that we are conscious of but a very small part of this vast cosmos? With the humility that our awareness of our limited scope must impose on us, our minds should be inspired to expand to ever wider explanations and greater possibilities, opening new frontiers of intellectual exploration.

Our awareness of the essence of an unseen order in the universe may always be faint. Attempts to understand it require a rigorous intellectual vitality and a willingness to absorb and discard mental constructs that hinder advancement. In a world in which time is cyclical, even a return to ancient ways of knowing, as Mayan cosmology posits, can be regarded as an advancement. It implies, and I strongly suggest William James would have agreed, that we can know something without knowing that we know it. A vast storehouse of "primitive" wisdom slumbers in the recesses of our mind—wherever the mind is thought to be located. And these ancient precepts argue that knowing something face to face, or through direct experience, is just the tip of the cognitive iceberg.

In the universe of possibilities, our belief system can atrophy us or enrich us. Belief can be regarded as the consent to something for which there may be no existing proof. Beliefs can blur clear distinctions between ideas and reality and so lay the groundwork for possibilities, what some might call miracles. Belief combined with imagination and a powerful emotional charge is potent medicine.

Thoughts or beliefs can activate related emotions, and emotions can alter physical realities, including our health. Hopeful beliefs can make us feel more vibrantly alive, and that sense of well-being can be translated to our bodies; it infects us in a positive way. As with current university studies of the placebo response, our thought processes clearly play a role in activating healing systems throughout the body. In this way, our cognitions and our assumed knowledge—and the related emotions—act in the same way as today's pharmaceuticals: in advance of swallowing them, we consent to their presumed effectiveness. Knowledge, belief, and healing go hand in hand in hand.

Perhaps the placebo effect can be epitomized by this recent example: In 2017, I visited an African shaman at his home, spending a week with his family. Throughout our time together, the shaman's wife, who had multiple physical and emotional maladies, kept observing me with keen interest. From her viewpoint, she saw something in me that could contribute to her recovery. One day, after she consulted with her talented husband, they approached and asked me to assist her.

"Why?" I asked.

Her response was profoundly insightful: "I believe in my beliefs. I have faith in faith. I believe in you, Gerry. I have faith in you, and I believe in myself. Let's work together."

That was the recipe for a healing, and, indeed, the results were seen in minutes and accumulated over days. She consulted with herself as much as she did with me. In tandem, the results seemed supernatural, but they were simply another example of the *super* in the *natural* that rests within us and all around us. In retrospect, it was her good fortune to have never met a scientist or physician who proclaimed her beliefs to be wrong.

Dualism is our natural way of assessing information, but if we are not familiar with its stifling effects, we may get stuck in a mental mud of our own making. Things that are known are often impediments to discovering the unknown, which, if realized, could then become the latest known. Knowledge and certainty too often close off uncertainty, imagination, and creativity. The certainty of knowing is more hazardous than not knowing; the latter may reflect an open-mindedness. Joseph Campbell cautioned us by saying, "The person who has found the ultimate truth is wrong."[3] Nobel Prize-winning physicist Niels Bohr opined that being logical is *not* thinking; it may be the mere recitation of today's set of facts.[4] Different ways of knowing are often seen as absolute and mutually excluding. Wrestling with contradictory viewpoints or competing hypotheses creates the mental discomfort known as cognitive dissonance, which can be a powerful fertilizer for intellectual growth. Opposite points of view can become regarded as complementary ideas. And as Goethe said, "What we agree with leaves us inactive, but contradictions make us productive."[5]

And then there is mystery—not knowing, not understanding; matters that have not yet even been contemplated can hold powerful healing force. As Einstein poignantly said, "I believe in mystery."[6] For those who do, intellectual and physical health seems boundless. Our questions of the great mysteries of Nature are more important than our meager answers. Nonsense, what could be regarded as the wildly inexplicable, often, in a stealthy and baffling way, unlocks the door to mysterious new insights. Often such ideas come at the edge of reality, perhaps in the dream world.

As I have seen during treks into the Amazon, shamans must be highly intuitive and inventive, especially in the absence of one-size-fits-all drugstore and hospital solutions. Perhaps we are seeing an increasing recognition of Siberian and jungle wisdom in the Western pursuit of many mind-expanding and mind-healing plant medicines such as psilocybin, ayahuasca, iboga, peyote, San Pedro, and their derivatives. Even animals are doing their part, as evidenced in the use of *kambo,* the immune-boosting secretions of jungle frogs or their cousins whose venom is used to treat opioid addiction in the Americas.

Much of what I have written in this book was, at some point in my career, mind-bending for me. Over the last fifteen years, my professional paradigms of understanding mental and physical illness have been steadily challenged. The esteemed Wade Davis, a Smithsonian anthropologist, is someone I have long held in high regard. He has asserted that every shaman will look a little crazy; that's their job. They enter into realities most of us don't even know exist and even talk to plants and deceased ancestors—or, worse yet, hear their voices. Are they delusional and suffering from hallucinations? From a Western perspective, many of them are regarded as suffering from what may be regarded as an exclusively hereditable form of schizophrenia and in need of mind-taming drugs. Yet, in fact, many tribal shamans can manage the psychotic process and because of their abilities are often regarded as holy men with an identifiable social role, when Western psychiatrists would try to diminish and suppress their "condition" with culturally narrow diagnoses and treatments. Or perhaps a missionary would come along and see this "afflicted" person and conclude that demons have taken over the shaman and an exorcism is in order. Shamans, Davis has always contended, walk a fine line between spirit possession, altered states, and enlightenment, while maintaining the ability to enter and depart these states at will.

Similarly, ayahuasqueros, shamans who regularly use ayahuasca as a healing medicine, often ingesting it daily, could easily be dismissed as being chemically dependent. And the tobaqueros who regularly snort or inhale nicotiania rustica for visionary support could be written off as having a tobacco-use disorder. Because many shamans lead a somewhat isolated existence, often living at the periphery of their communities, a psychiatrist may label them as suffering from an avoidant personality disorder, or, given their odd-appearing ways, perhaps they could be stigmatized with the diagnosis of schizoid personality disorder.

A homosexual man in Native American culture was traditionally known as a *two-spirit*. A male-bodied person who dressed in the attire of a woman—what psychologists would diagnose as a transvestite—was commonly interpreted as having special visionary gifts. And as a variant of the two-spirited, he was individually suited to be a powerful shaman and visionary who was often in the frontlines, leading his people into warfare to assure their safety. In other words, they were not suffering from any kind of psychological disturbance; they were gifted and acknowledged as such and fulfilled special leadership roles in their cultures.

An ecstatic male-bodied dancer in female attire participating in an African Venda ceremony may dance the night through in a traditional welcoming ceremony. That might puzzle a visiting psychologist from Des Moines. On the surface, the dancer's actions might look like mania, perhaps symptomatic of an untreated bipolar disorder. Or maybe he's a narcissist. From the Venda perspective, though, the gender-fluid dancer is simply a revered member of the community, a ceremonialist who guides and enlivens reverent events.

FIGURE 14. Welcoming Ceremony, Venda Tribe, South Africa. The gender-fluid man can be seen dancing in the left foreground. (Author's photograph)

Heyokas, a kind of sacred clown in the Native American Lakota culture, were common on the American Plains. They behaved peculiarly and provoked a lot of laughter. Sometimes their clothing was disarranged, or they rode a horse sitting backward. Often their attire and behavior were opposite from or contrary to the rest of the culture. Perhaps a heyoka would publicly wash his hands with dust as confounded children watched, only to feel subconsciously prompted to go to a stream and rinse themselves off before returning home to eat after a long day of play. So how would we diagnose heyokas today? At minimum, as nonconforming malcontents. Perhaps as prepsychotic, just about ready to "lose it." If, however, a heyoka were to don a suit and tie and get licensed as a professional counselor, we might revere him as a shrewd, paradoxical therapist who provides novel and indirect ways to motivate the patient to address a problem.

Certainly, if a shaman used sleight-of-hand surgical techniques or placebo medicines while visiting the United States, he could easily be arrested and prosecuted. Meanwhile, his colleague in Peru might be revered as an astonishing healer. In contrast, when I have explained to shamans how Western psychiatrists treat opioid addictions by prescribing much more addictive opioids, all the while ignoring the life-saving possibilities of the iboga root, they are astonished by our primitive, nonsensical, if not cruel, customs.

The limits of our languages limit understanding the world. Our scientific way of knowing and naming is often a constraint to intellectual growth. How we observe affects *what* we observe. Just when we think we have an understanding of events, the confusion quickly resumes. Just when truths appear to have been discovered and we rigorously categorize them, along comes a Bushman to say, "I cannot tell you the truth; I can only tell you what I know from my experience." Common sense in one culture is often viewed as uncommon nonsense in another.

So, what am I suggesting you do with all these culturally rich and contrasting illustrations? First, that you savor them without too much judgment. Perhaps you will create the mental space to entertain the notion that amid all our rich cultural diversity there is an underlying unity that is just dressed up a bit differently depending on the context. And with that internal adjustment, a greater sense of harmony and health is inclined to emerge. In the Venezuelan jungle, it is difficult to find a Yanomami tribal member who proclaims to be a Republican or a Democrat, a Protestant or a Catholic. In fact, many Yanomami don't even have a name. So, the first core teaching that indigenous people offer us is to be in the world in another way.

This leads us to the second teaching: Celebrate life by being more communal and less self-absorbed. It is important to be a nondescript contributor to the community of humanity and beyond. We are to reweave our life into the greater tapestry.

Appendix

Techniques Used in Juan Fidel's Healing Ceremony

Chapter 3, *"Health Crisis in the Amazon,"* recounts my visit to the Achuar tribe in Ecuador when the local shaman told me to heal Juan Fidel, who had fallen in his canoe a week earlier and was now suffering from severe head trauma. The painful pressure from the likely swelling of his brain had prevented him from urinating or defecating for days, forcing him to stop eating and drinking. It seemed clear that, without help, he would soon die.

Leading up to my work with Juan was a dream I had in which my deceased father was healed from Parkinson's disease. The following morning, recounting that dream led to a rapid "downloading" of messages I experienced as I sat next to Juan. Like a *knowing*, these messages arrived bereft of language in a sensory way unlike anything I had experienced before. They informed me in detail exactly what elements the healing needed to orchestrate. I summarize these intuited "marching instructions" here.

1. Be Introduced by an Authority Figure

The day before the healing, I had accompanied the tribe's revered shaman, Rafael, to a sacred waterfall, snorted his dream tobacco, and, with him, convened with the ancestors and power animals. Then I had had the dream of my own father's healing. These events led Rafael to endorse my legitimacy, healing abilities, and enhanced power to the tribe. This endorsement by the chief authority figure created *hope* and *expectations* for change in both Juan and the community. Rafael expressed complete confidence in my ability: he advised me to heal Juan Fidel and abruptly walked away.

2. Assemble a Community of Supporters

The message was that I was to encircle Juan with a cadre of smiling and optimistic supporters. This would raise *shamanic potentiation*: the power of two being like the presence of four, the power of four being eight, and so on, disproportionately raising the energy level. Additionally, it might create a *social contagion* health effect if every person displayed hope and optimism in the presence of one another.

3. Open the Healing Ceremony with a Gratitude Ritual

Rituals help to create *sacred space*, provide an *emotional signature* to the event, and impart a *suggestion of change* of what was about to occur. Prayer and meditation of thanks were to be offered for the healing that was about to unfold, *increasing expectations*. Initially, I was to remove *obstacles to healing*, such as fear and despair, clearing the way for change. Next, I was to summon the favor and support of Pachamama by giving before receiving—in this case, a ritual offering of tobacco and chicha.

4. **Create Positive Imagery**

All participants were to be asked to share a *unified vision* of Juan Fidel being healed. Prayers were not to involve pleading, imploring, or begging for recovery, as this could bring negative energy into the circle. The community was to be instructed eagerly to imagine Juan as fully recovered—healthy, vigorous, robust, and smiling. Then we were to watch for it to happen.

5. **Bring a Smile to the Patient's Face**

The message was for me to ask Juan to imagine a family member who had the broadest and most contagious smile—in this case, his beloved eldest son. Then Juan was momentarily to wear that smile himself. This technique was intended to "trick" his body, via *sacred magic*, into a cavalcade of physiological changes, all advancing him in the direction of restoration and healing (*epigenetics*).

6. **Touch and Make Eye Contact**

I was instructed to allow Juan to see and feel my calm, confidence, and loving care as displayed by direct *eye contact* (much as in a *mirror-neuron effect*) and *gentle, authoritative touch*. This technique could further remove additional obstacles to healing such as loneliness, separation from family, and feelings of helplessness. I was to provide a constant tactile reminder that someone strong was present to help him.

7. **Change/Shift Energy**

The message was to provide head-to-head shivering or convulsing to change Juan's internal vibrational energy immediately and dramatically, moving him out of his stuck spot. And I was to add unusual sounds (e.g., chanting, and humming) to do the same—*shifting vibrational patterns.*

8. Create Heart Resonance/Heart Aesthesis

Much as I had learned from the Himba tribe of Nimibia, I felt guided to connect the electrical energy of Juan's heart with mine. Physical closeness and heartfelt concern would transmit my care, serenity, and strength. Patient and healer would subtly merge as one, the *dominant energy* being a healing calm.

9. Synchronize Breathing

I was informed that deep breathing would promote additional relaxation. This ritualized activity was intended to transport Juan to a new emotional place. It would further serve to unite healer and patient. This process would *change the internal state* and *focus of attention,* shifting Juan from previously frightening thoughts and physical pain to more neutral and less disturbing emotions.

10. Add Mystery

I was to guide Juan to chant with me in a foreign tongue (more *sacred magic* blended with *imagination*) to raise his vibrational level. Together, the two of us would look upward to the distant sun and invite the limitless powers of Nature to participate, thereby planting the seed thought that anything is possible in this extraordinarily vast and largely unknown universe. The wisdom is that for whatever problem befalls us on the earth, there is a complementary remedy to be found around us, perhaps in previously uninvestigated places.

11. Administer Placebos

My guidance was that inert agents could provide additional suggestion and sacred magic. I was to encourage Juan to anticipate positive changes within a short time. Administration of this medicine would raise the likelihood of a positive shift in the direction of health—a *placebo effect*. The process was intended to awaken Juan's *inner doctor*. The placebo would be muti already in my possession (vitamin C and CoQ10 capsules in my backpack—the "medicine bag").

12. Give Thanks to Close the Sacred Healing Ceremony

An additional prayer of gratitude near the end of the ceremony was to be added to punctuate the observed results, to *concretize* them. This created a "sandwich effect" of sorts— gratitude at both ends. The group would communally express thanks for the healing that was almost complete, a near final *emotional signature* that "all is well."

13. Convene an Evening Extraction Ceremony

The message was to remove bodily invaders—*tsentsak*— via sucking and spitting.[1] In Juan's case, this curative was administered by Rafael, who extracted the cause of illness from Juan's body into his own phlegm and discarded it onto the earth. The healing was to conclude with the ingestion of ayahuasca further to move illness from the body.

Notes

Introduction

1. *Set* and *setting* are two of the factors that make for a healing experience. *Set* describes the psychological environment in which a medicine is ingested, serving as a safe and sacred container grounded in solid values and good intentions. In other words, the medicine is consumed not for mere fun or recreation but to delve into spiritual realms. Users must be clear that they are using the medicine in this spiritual way.

   While *set* thus speaks to motivation, *setting* describes the physical location. Sitting in the back seat of a car to get stoned, for instance, would be a wrong setting; ingesting medicine under supervision in a clinic would be a proper one.

Chapter 3

1. C. G. Jung, *Collected Works*, vol. 10, *Civilization in Transition*, quoted in Anthony Stevens, The *Two Million-Year-Old Self* (College Station, TX: Texas A & M University Press 1993), 3.

Chapter 4

1. Bradford Keeney, *The Bushman Way of Tracking God* (New York: Simon & Schuster, 2010), 72.
2. Ibid., 7.
3. Ibid., 224.

Chapter 5

1. Sigurd F. Olson, quoted in David Backes, ed., *Spirit of the North: The Quotable Sigurd F. Olson* (Minneapolis: University of Minnesota Press, 2004), 53. Backes found the quote in a newspaper article Olson wrote in the *Minneapolis Star-Journal* on April 20, 1941, entitled "Spring Morning."
2. Sigurd F. Olson, *The Singing Wilderness* (Minneapolis: University of Minnesota Press, 1997), 82–83.
3. Richard Gerber MD, *A Practical Guide to Vibrational Medicine* (Rochester, VT: Bear & Company, 2001), 494.

Chapter 6

1. Adapted from the author's interview of Clint Ober, "Giving Voice to Mother Earth," *Sacred Hoop* 81 (2013): 6–11.

Chapter 7

1. Terror management theory was originally proposed by Jeff Greenberg, Sheldon Solomon, and Tom Pyszczynski in *The Worm at the Core: On the Role of Death in Life* (London: Penguin/Allen Lane, 2015).

Chapter 8

1. Josh Axe, *Eat Dirt* (New York: Harper, 2016).

Chapter 9

1. Martin Luther King, Jr.'s full quote is, "One day we shall win freedom, but not only for ourselves. We shall so appeal to your heart and conscience that we shall win you in the process, and our victory will be a double victory." Retrieved from azquotes.com/author/8044-Martin_Luther_King_Jr/tag/victory.
2. Rupert Ross, *Returning to the Teachings: Exploring Aboriginal Justice* (Toronto: Penguin, 1996), 104.
2. Ibid., 190.

Chapter 10

1. This idea comes from David Rockwell, author of *Giving Voice to Bear* (Toronto: Key Porter Books, 1991). I've scoured the text but can't find any reference to the specific word; he speaks generally.

Chapter 11

1. Rick Strassman, MD, *DMT: The Spirit Molecule* (Rochester, VT: Park Street Press, 2001), 53–55.
2. Personal conversation between patient and author.
3. Rollo May, *Love and Will* (Toronto: George J. McLeod, Ltd. 1969), 243.

Chapter 13

1. Robert Augustus Masters, *Spiritual Bypassing: When Spirituality Disconnects Us from What Really Matters* (Berkeley: North Atlantic Press, 2010), 196.
2. John Muir, *My First Summer in the Sierra* (Boston: Houghton Mifflin, 1911), 157–8.
3. Erwin Shröedinger, *AZQuotes*; retrieved from https://www.azquotes.com/quote/1117697.
4. See Alan Eriera, *The Elder Brothers: A Lost South American People and Their Message about the Fate of the Earth* (New York: Vintage Books, 1993).
5. Although this statement is attributed to Yeats and Bertrand Russell, it is actually from Eden Phillpotts, *A Shadow Passes* (London: Cecil Palmer & Hayward, 1918), 19.
6. Joseph Chilton Pearce, *The Biology of Transcendence: A Blueprint of the Human Spirit* (Rochester, VT: Park Street Press, 2004), 110–111.
7. Ibid.
8. Organismic theorist Kurt Goldstein introduced the term *self-actualization* to describe an organism's motive to realize its full potential: "The tendency to actualize itself as fully as possible is the basic drive . . . the drive of self-actualization." Kurt Goldstein, quoted in Arnold H. Modell, *The Private Self* (Cambridge, MA: Harvard University Press, 1993), 44.

Chapter 14

1. Kurt Anderson, "How America Lost Its Mind," *The Atlantic* (September 2017): 78.
2. Maggie Jackson, *Distracted: Reclaiming Our Focus in a World of Lost Attention* (New York: Prometheus, 2009), 14.

3. Susan Pinkler, *The Village Effect: How Face-to-Face Contact Can Make Us Healthier, Happier, and Smarter* (New York: Spiegel & Grau, 2014), 6.

4. See Pinkler, *Village Effect*; Kenneth Pelletier, *Longevity: Fulfilling Our Biological Potential* (New York: Delacorte Press, 1982); and Wayne Jonas, *How Healing Works: Get Well and Stay Well Using Your Hidden Power to Heal* (New York: Lorena Jones Books, 2018).

5. José Stevens, PhD, with Lena Stevens, *The Power Path: The Shaman's Way to Success in Business and Life* (Novato, CA: New World Library, 2002), 188.

6. Martin Prechtel, *Long Life, Honey in the Heart: A Story of Initiation and Eloquence from the Shores of a Mayan Lake* (New York: Tarcher/Putnam, 1999), 140.

7. Ibid., 132.

8. Ibid.

9. Mahatma Gandhi, "Prayer in Gandhi's Ashram," *Mahatma Gandhi's Writings, Philosophy, Audio, Video & Photographs*, retrieved from https://www.mkgandhi.org/prayer.htm.

Conclusion

1. Dan and Chip Heath, "Why Second Life Failed," *Slate* (Nov 8, 2011); retrieved from https://slate.com/business/2011/11/why-second-life-failed-how-the-milkshake-test-helps-predict-which-ultrahyped-technology-will-succeed-and-which-wont.html.

2. William James, *Pragmatism and Other Writings* (New York: Penguin Classics, 2000), 190–91.

3. Joseph Campbell, *The Power of Myth* (New York: Doubleday, 1988), 55.

4. Neil Bohr, quoted in William Glen, ed., *Mass Extinction Debates: How Science Works in a Crisis* (Redwood City, CA: Stanford University Press, 1994), 62.

5. Johann Wolfgang von Goethe, quoted in E. A. Bucchianeri, *Faust: My Soul Be Damned for the World, Vol. 2* (Bloomington, IN: AuthorHouse, 2008), 654.

5. Albert Einstein, *The World as I See It* (Minneapolis: Filiquarian Publishing, 2006) 5.

Appendix

1. Chapter 3 describes tsentsak as magical darts to be installed into the body for healing. Their use as described in the appendix seems contradictory, for here the tsentsak are seen as damaging bodily invaders that must be removed. The contradiction is resolved, though, when we view the nature of tsentsak as paradoxical and multidimensional. We can think of them as a force or energy that can cause problems but can also remove them, just as medicines can be helpful or dangerous depending on how they are used. Tsentsak are damaging invaders when they cause illness, but in another form they can flush illness out.

Selected Bibliography

Anderson, Kurt. "How America Lost Its Mind." *The Atlantic* (September 2017): 78.

Arden, Nicky. *African Spirits Speak*. Rochester, VT: Destiny Books, 1999.

Axe, Josh. *Eat Dirt*. New York: Harper, 2016.

Backes, David, ed. *Spirit of the North: The Quotable Sigurd F. Olson*. Minneapolis: University of Minnesota Press, 2004.

Blanchard, Geral. "Giving Voice to Mother Earth." *Sacred Hoop* 81 (2013): 6–11.

Bourzat, Françoise. *Consciousness Medicine*. Berkeley, CA: North Atlantic Press, 2019.

Cumes, David, MD. *Africa in my Bones*. Cape Town, South Africa: New Africa Books, 2004.

Cumes, David. *The Spirit of Healing*. St. Paul, MN: Llewellyn Publications, 1999.

Gerber, Richard. *A Practical Guide to Vibrational Medicine*. Rochester, VT: Bear & Company, 2001.

Greenberg, Jeff, Sheldon Solomon, and Tom Pyszczynski. *The Worm at the Core: On the Role of Death in Life*. London: Penguin/Allen Lane, 2015.

Hall, James. *Sangoma*. New York: Jeremy P. Tarcher/Putnam Books, 1994.

Jackson, Maggie. *Distracted: Reclaiming Our Focus in a World of Lost Attention*. New York: Prometheus, 2009.

Jonas, Wayne. *How Healing Works: Get Well and Stay Well Using Your Hidden Power to Heal*. New York: Lorena Jones Books, 2018.

Keeney, Bradford. *The Bushman Way of Tracking God*. New York: Simon & Schuster, 2010.

Masters, Robert Augustus. *Spiritual Bypassing: When Spirituality Disconnects Us from What Really Matters*. Berkeley: North Atlantic Press, 2010.

Muir, John. *My First Summer in the Sierra*. Boston: Houghton Mifflin, 1911.

Ober, Clinton. *Earthing* (2nd ed). Laguna Beach, CA: Basic Health Publications, 2014.

Olson, Sigurd. *The Singing Wilderness*. Minneapolis: University of Minnesota Press, 1997.

Pearce, Joseph Chilton. *The Biology of Transcendence: A Blueprint of the Human Spirit*. Rochester, VT: Park Street Press, 2004.

Pelletier, Kenneth. *Longevity: Fulfilling Our Biological Potential*. New York: Delacorte Press, 1982.

Pinkler, Susan. *The Village Effect: How Face-to-Face Contact Can Make Us Healthier, Happier, and Smarter*. New York: Spiegel & Grau, 2014.

Prechtel, Martin. *Long Life, Honey in the Heart: A Story of Initiation and Eloquence from the Shores of a Mayan Lake.* New York: Tarcher/Putnam, 1999.

Rockwell, David. *Giving Voice to Bear.* Toronto: Key Porter Books, 1991.

Ross, Rupert. *Returning to the Teachings: Exploring Aboriginal Justice.* Toronto: Penguin, 1996.

Stevens, José, PhD, with Lena Stevens. *The Power Path: The Shaman's Way to Success in Business and Life.* Novato, CA: New World Library, 2002.

Strassman, Rick, MD. *DMT: The Spirit Molecule.* Rochester, VT: Park Street Press, 2001.

About the Author

Geral Blanchard, LPC, BCCP, NCP, has enjoyed the privilege of serving patients in a psychotherapeutic setting over several decades. His professional career began in the field of child abuse, and later he addressed both sides of the equation—abusers as well as victims. Gerry has worked in a variety of settings as a consultant assessing violent individuals including rapists, lust murderers, and serial killers.

With training in anthropology and psychology, Gerry has become increasingly appreciative of the diverse ways in which antipodal cultures respond to trauma, addictions, abusive behavior, and other seemingly irreparable physical maladies. In the last decade, his practice has shifted focus to incorporate indigenous healing wisdom into contemporary treatment models impacting a wide variety of patients.

Gerry has observed and worked alongside shamans and sangomas in a variety of locations: South Africa, Zimbabwe, Tanzania, Swaziland, Rwanda, Nicaragua, Guatemala, Colombia, Peru, Ecuador, Canada, and the United States. He has participated in many indigenous rituals and ceremonies that incorporate plant medicines into the healing process. This experience has given him a strong interest in the efficacy of psychedelic medicines, especially when introduced in sacred treatment settings.

Gerry has a psychotherapy office in Des Moines, Iowa, and can be reached at blanchardgeral@gmail.com.

CPSIA information can be obtained
at www.ICGtesting.com
Printed in the USA
LVHW011014130520
655433LV00012B/267